The Quaker Faith

The Quaker Faith

Friends of Love and Truth

Stuart K. Masters

NEW YORK • LONDON • OXFORD • NEW DELHI • SYDNEY

T&T CLARK

Bloomsbury Publishing Inc, 1359 Broadway, New York, NY 10018, USA
Bloomsbury Publishing Plc, 50 Bedford Square, London, WC1B 3DP, UK
Bloomsbury Publishing Ireland, 29 Earlsfort Terrace, Dublin 2, D02 AY28, Ireland

BLOOMSBURY, T&T CLARK and the T&T Clark logo are trademarks of
Bloomsbury Publishing Plc

First published in the United States of America 2025

Copyright © Bloomsbury Publishing, Inc 2025

For legal purposes the Acknowledgments on p. viii constitute an extension
of this copyright page.

Cover design: Diana Nuhn
Cover image © iStock.com/Peter_Horvath

All rights reserved. No part of this publication may be: i) reproduced or transmitted in any form, electronic or mechanical, including photocopying, recording or by means of any information storage or retrieval system without prior permission in writing from the publishers; or ii) used or reproduced in any way for the training, development or operation of artificial intelligence (AI) technologies, including generative AI technologies. The rights holders expressly reserve this publication from the text and data mining exception as per Article 4(3) of the Digital Single Market Directive (EU) 2019/790.

Bloomsbury Publishing Inc does not have any control over, or responsibility for, any third-party websites referred to or in this book. All internet addresses given in this book were correct at the time of going to press. The author and publisher regret any inconvenience caused if addresses have changed or sites have ceased to exist, but can accept no responsibility for any such changes.

Library of Congress Cataloging-in-Publication Data

ISBN: HB: 978-1-5381-8534-6
PB: 978-1-5381-8535-3
ePDF: 979-8-8818-6131-5
eBook: 978-1-5381-8536-0

Typeset by Deanta Global Publishing Services, Chennai, India

For product safety related questions contact productsafety@bloomsbury.com.

To find out more about our authors and books visit www.bloomsbury.com and sign up for our newsletters.

Take heed, dear Friends, to the promptings of love and truth in your hearts, which are the leadings of God.[1]

---

[1] London Yearly Meeting, *Advices and Queries* (London: London Yearly Meeting, 1964), 9.

Contents

Acknowledgements	viii
Introduction	1

Part One   History and Development

1	The Roots: Quaker Foundations	9
2	The Branches: Quaker Diversity	35

Part Two   Spirituality and Practice

3	The Inward: Quaker Worship and Spiritual Practice	65
4	The Testing: Quaker Discernment and Decision-Making	91
5	The Outward: Quaker Testimony	107

Part Three   Contribution and Challenges

6	The Quaker Spiritual Journey	133
7	The Critical Friend: Reviewing the Quaker Experience	147
	Epilogue	167

Glossary	175
Bibliography	179
Index	186
About the Author	193

Acknowledgements

I am immensely grateful to my Woodbrooke colleagues, past and present, and especially to those who have directly supported my research and teaching over the years, including Timothy Peat Ashworth, Simon Best, 'Ben' Pink Dandelion, Michael Eccles, Maud Grainger, Rhiannon Grant, Douglas Gwyn, Betty Hagglund, Mart Layton, Helen Rowlands, Mark Russ, and Simonne Wood. Also, to the many course participants I have worked with, whose interesting and challenging responses have contributed to my own learning.

In planning and writing this book, I have appreciated the invaluable guidance and support offered by Margery Post Abbott, Beth Allen, Paul Anderson, Margaret Benefiel, Tiffany Berman, Brent Bill, Cherice Bock, Pink Dandelion, Jon Kershner, Marcelle Martin, Anna Masters, Myra Skipper, and Dan Yarnell. Richard Brown and Victoria Shi at Bloomsbury have been kind, responsive, and a joy to work with. Finally, for all their love and encouragement, I owe a huge debt of gratitude to my family, Anna and Joey, Harriet, Stephaan and Ava, Emily, Elisha, Olive and Derek, Josephine and Russ, as well as the wider Berman, Gittens, Haynes, Klassen, and Statham families.

Introduction

What does the word "Quaker" conjure up in your mind? Perhaps it makes you think of the Quaker Oats Company and the figure of a jolly man in eighteenth-century garb who appears on the packaging of their products. The word can often invoke images of a quaint and peculiar people from the past, with men in distinctive hats and women wearing bonnets. Today, however, a Quaker is more likely to be a young African Evangelical Christian, or perhaps a middle-aged American humanist who practices Buddhist meditation. Quakers, or Friends as they have traditionally called themselves, have been around for over three hundred and fifty years, a Protestant group rooted in Christianity that emerged out of the turmoil of the English Civil Wars and the short-lived English Republic. At the present time, they remain a relatively small but diverse community with a genuinely global presence. However, despite their modest numbers, some four hundred thousand people across the world today, in a range of different ways they have made a considerable impact on the modern world, especially within Great Britain, Ireland, and North America. We can see this influence, for example, in the areas of business, the sciences, education, philanthropy, and social reform. In England, during the eighteenth and nineteenth centuries, Friends played an important part in the development of the Industrial Revolution. The Darby family of Coalbrookdale pioneered modern approaches to iron ore smelting with the invention of the blast furnace, and the Pease family of Darlington established the first steam railway line from Stockton to Darlington. They also became extremely successful in the commercial sector, and many Quaker businesses from this time are still well-known names today including the banks, Lloyds, Barclays, and Sandy Spring; the confectioners, Cadbury, Fry, and Rowntree;

biscuit-makers, Carr's, Huntley & Palmers, and Jacob's; shoemakers, Clarks; and lawyers, Duane Morris. Friends have made their mark in medicine and the sciences. John Fothergill achieved important advances in disease control, and Joseph Lister was a pioneer of antiseptic surgery. Notable figures in modern science include the physicists John Dalton and Ursula Franklin, and the astrophysicists Arthur Eddington and Jocelyn Bell Burnell. In the United States, there are many educational institutions with Quaker roots, such as Johns Hopkins and George Fox Universities, and Earlham, Guilford, Haverford, and Swarthmore Colleges. Friends are also known for their philanthropic and social reform work, particularly in the areas of abolitionism, housing, mental health, peacebuilding, penal reform, and temperance, and were involved in the formation of several contemporary charities and campaign groups, such as Amnesty International, Greenpeace, and Oxfam.

The spiritual heritage of Quakers is both distinctive and intriguing. Friends are not easily categorized, as they express a diverse range of beliefs and practices, from Evangelical Christians to Buddhists, Pagans, and Nontheists. Their origin within English Puritanism suggests a Reformed Protestant orientation, but some aspects of their faith look more Catholic. On the one hand, they took the general trajectory of the Protestant Reformation to its logical conclusion, not just simplifying worship and ceremony, but doing away with external liturgy and imagery altogether. At the same time, their contemplative worship practice, approach to the Bible, belief in the inward presence of Christ, and emphasis on holiness meant that, in the seventeenth century, they were often accused of being Catholics in disguise. In more recent times, a form of worship based on stillness and silence enabled some Friends to form multi-faith and multi-belief communities. At root, the Quaker way seems to be part of a dissenting stream of Western Christianity represented by medieval movements of popular piety, groups on the radical wing of the European Reformation, and separatist sects emerging out of the English Revolution. Friends share a family resemblance with the various Anabaptist groups, such as the Mennonites, Hutterites, and Church of the Brethren, and, along with them, make up the Historic Peace Church tradition, which has regarded a rejection of war and other forms of physical violence as an essential feature of Christian discipleship. Perhaps what is most distinctive about Quaker spirituality is the attention Friends have always given to the possibility of directly receiving and acting on divine revelation and guidance both as a community and as individuals. This is the principal focus of their communal worship and spiritual practices. Such an approach has produced a distinctive faith and practice based on three key elements. Firstly, Friends commit themselves to the inward work of being attentive to the Spirit of God so that they can experience a sense of being guided. Secondly, once such divine guidance has been received, they must carefully interrogate and test where it is leading them through a rigorous discipline of discernment. Thirdly, having come to a position of clearness about where God is leading, they seek to undertake the outward work of being adventurous and being faithful in putting into practice what God has called them to do. This three-stage process is followed on an ongoing basis throughout their lives and in all their different roles, responsibilities, and activities. This book takes a detailed yet accessible look at this fascinating faith tradition and considers how and why Quakers have claimed to be Friends of love and truth; reviews Quaker history; examines how Friends have changed over time; and undertakes a careful study of Quaker spirituality as a pathway that involves being attentive, being guided, being discerning, being adventurous, and being faithful. It helps explain the significant impact that Friends have made on the modern world, as champions of freedom of conscience, peace, and social justice. The book is divided into three parts.

The two chapters making up part one consider the history and development of the Quaker way over the past four centuries. Chapter 1 explores Quaker beginnings, the religious and political context out of which Friends emerged, the essential characteristics of early Quaker faith and practice, and how this established a complex legacy for future generations to negotiate. Chapter 2 traces the development and diversification of the Quaker community over time, including the struggle to survive severe persecution in the seventeenth century, the formation of a peculiar people who were spiritually separated but socially and economically engaged in the eighteenth century, the impact of the Evangelical movement which led to conflict, shattering their unity and producing new expressions of the Quaker faith in the nineteenth century, finishing with the remarkable success of global missions, and the rise of Liberal and Pluralist Quakerism in the twentieth century.

The three chapters in part two examine the key features of Quaker spirituality. Chapter 3 explores the inward work of Quaker worship and spiritual practice, which aims to nurture a deepening sense of God's presence and an experience of divine guidance. It discusses how Friends order their worship, traditional forms of Quaker spiritual practice, innovations associated with the development of Pastoral and Evangelical Quakerism, and what worship and spiritual practice mean within Liberal and Pluralist Quaker communities. It also considers several metaphors that help us gain a fuller appreciation of Quaker experience and practice. Chapter 4 examines how Friends make decisions in a worshipful way, using a discipline of discernment, in which they interrogate and test their motivations and emotional responses in seeking God's will. It explores key processes and practices Friends use in doing this discernment and in making decisions both as a community and as individuals. Chapter 5 focuses on the outward work of putting divine guidance into action, once it has been received and discerned. Friends have called this lived aspect of their faith their "testimony" or "witness," and it has usually been interpreted as an embodied expression of the peace, integrity, and justice of Jesus. It reflects on the overall shape and orientation of Quaker testimony and considers how this has been enacted in different circumstances and at various times across history.

Part three is made up of two chapters that identify and assess what the Quaker way has to offer and the challenges and limitations Friends have experienced in practice. Chapter 6 follows the various stages and pathways associated with the Quaker spiritual journey, guided by the writings of a range of contemporary Friends. If the Bible begins with the creation story and ends with a vision of a new creation, the Quaker spiritual journey starts with a discomforting sense that all is not well with the world, prompting Friends to set out on a pilgrimage in search of the new creation. Chapter 7 surveys some of the challenges and limitations Friends have encountered in seeking to live the Quaker way within the world. This includes (1) an assessment of several dynamic tensions that have made it difficult for Friends to maintain a balanced faith and (2) an examination of some specific situations in which Quakers have failed to live up to the high ethical standards they profess. Finally, a brief epilogue reviews the material covered, assesses the prospects of the Quaker tradition in all its global contexts and diversity, and considers what Friends have to offer a world facing an uncertain and precarious future.

In this book, I have attempted to write an introduction to the Quaker way that is accessible but also comprehensive and rigorous. The balance between accessibility and rigor is not easily achieved. Given that the text includes some technical language, I have included a glossary divided into two parts. The first part covers significant terms used in Christian doctrine and theology, while the other provides an index of Quaker jargon. I hope you find this glossary helpful as you work through the book. In addition, the endnotes and the bibliography indicate opportunities to explore key subjects or themes in more detail, should you wish to do so. A comprehensive set of learning resources are also available for free download from my website—www.stuartkmasters.com.

Part One

History and Development

1

The Roots

Quaker Foundations

The Religious Context

The Quaker movement emerged out of a radical religious and political culture that had taken shape over the previous centuries.

Late Medieval Popular Piety

Major social and political change during the late medieval period (1200–1500), including urbanization, the development of nation-states, wars, and plagues, led to growing criticism of the perceived corruptions of the wealthy and powerful Catholic Church. One response to these changes among the general population was a desire to live a life of piety, modeled on the example of Jesus and the apostles. This became known as the *vita apostolica* (the apostolic life). The Catholic Church viewed a commitment to voluntary poverty and service as a special vocation to be followed only within recognized religious orders. However, those committed to the *vita apostolica* refused to withdraw to the monastery and asserted that their way of life should be the norm for all true Christian believers, not just the few. The Church saw this as a challenge to its authority, resulting in conflict, accusations of heresy, and persecution. The *vita apostolica* movement included groups, such as the Beguines, the Spiritual Franciscans, and the *Devotio Moderna*, often influenced by the

Rhineland mysticism of Meister Eckhart, Johannes Tauler, and Henry Suso. These early developments helped set the scene for the European Reformation, which took place during the first half of the sixteenth century.

The European Reformation

Initially, the demand for religious reform focused on practical matters of Catholic institutional corruption, such as the misuse of money and the selling of indulgences.[1] However, as reformers such as Martin Luther and John Calvin, with the support of their local rulers, separated their churches from Rome, they developed new doctrines that clearly distinguished Protestants from the Catholicism they were rejecting. Perhaps most important was the way the authority of the Bible was elevated above the tradition of the Church in religious life and practice. The reformers asserted the absolute sovereignty of God in the salvation process and played down any active role for individuals and the organized Church. Salvation was the work of God alone, and people simply had to have faith in God's promises and in the atoning work of Christ, as these were described in the Scriptures.[2] Worship among Protestants became focused on reading and preaching on the Bible, rather than participating in the liturgies and sacraments of the Catholic Church. To their opponents, this seemed to widen the gulf between God and humanity and produced a more pessimistic view of human nature and the possibility of transformation in this life. While the Holy Spirit was available to believers, this did not necessarily imply the presence of Christ. The Spirit was merely a helper and guide, particularly in the interpretation of the Scriptures. Finally, because all the mainstream reformers depended on the protection of their local civic powers, they continued to support the principle of a state–Church alliance.

These events provoked demands for more far-reaching political and religious changes, leading to the German Peasants' War (1524-5) and the emergence of movements calling for radical reform. In opposition to the mainstream reformers, the radicals rejected the Christendom idea that people were Christian simply by being born into a particular territory. Instead, they emphasized the need to make a voluntary commitment based on an experience of conversion. While accepting the authority of the Bible, these radicals gave greater emphasis to the Holy Spirit as the key agent of conversion and spiritual regeneration. They acknowledged that salvation was by faith alone, but understood this more in terms of an intimate inward relationship with God in Spirit, than the mere profession of belief. True Christianity meant discipleship, following in the footsteps of Christ and revealing the divine nature in one's life. They demanded greater reform of the faith than the mainstream reformers were prepared to accept and were unwilling to abandon many of the practices of popular piety associated with the late medieval *vita apostolica* movement. To the rich and powerful, such a commitment to the separation of Church and state, particularly when combined with calls for political and economic reform, represented a serious threat to the social order, and the radical groups experienced brutal persecution within both Catholic and Protestant jurisdictions. The two most significant movements on the radical wing of the Reformation were the Anabaptists and the Spiritualists. The early Anabaptists, whose various denominations later became part of the historic peace churches,[3] embodied a radically Christ-centered form of discipleship based on the Sermon on the Mount.[4] The faith of the Spiritualists focused on an inward encounter with God that did not depend upon any external sacraments or liturgies. There were complex interconnections between these two groups, and the Anabaptists had their own Spiritualist wing.

The English Reformation and Puritanism

The English Reformation of the 1530s was different in character from its European counterpart. Henry VIII had no interest in religious reform and separated the Church of England from the Roman Catholic Church primarily for personal and political reasons. Nevertheless, these events had far-reaching consequences for the religious life of England. In the following hundred years, the Monarchy and the Church hierarchy maintained traditional episcopal structures and enacted only moderate doctrinal and liturgical reforms. In response, the Puritans worked to "purify" the English Church of all remnants of Roman Catholicism and reform it based on Calvinist principles. This meant asserting the absolute authority of the Bible and affirming the Calvinist doctrine of double predestination, which is the belief that God has elected some people for eternal salvation and others for eternal punishment. This meant that the spiritual destiny of individuals was entirely dependent on decisions that God had already made.

In the early seventeenth century, a radical form of Puritanism emerged in England that caused significant conflict within the Puritan community.[5] The evidence suggests that this movement drew inspiration from religious writings from European Radical reformers, including a wide range of mystical, spiritualist, and Anabaptist sources. In opposition to the Calvinists, these Radical Puritans shared a number of common tendencies: (1) the belief that the old outward religious law had been abolished and replaced by the inward guidance of the Holy Spirit; (2) the rejection of external sacraments and ceremonies, viewed as the idolatrous worship of physical things rather than God; (3) a practice of total passivity and surrender before God, rather than the more active disciplines of mainstream Puritan piety; (4) the assertion that liberation from sin was possible in this life through the freely given grace of God; and (5) a conviction that salvation was universally available through the gift of the Holy Spirit.[6] So, in place of the deep spiritual anxiety associated with predestination, these radicals offered a real sense of assurance and joy in the present, and they found that a life of holiness flowed naturally from their inward experiences. Crucial to all of this seems to have been a real conviction that Christ was now returning in Spirit to dwell within his people. The London Radical Puritan preacher, John Everarde (1584–1641), wrote:

> To see Christ to be all in all in us, that is to know him experimentally; and if you know him thus, then you know him as you ought to know him, else he is but a fable to you; for so to know him is to have all the Scriptures fulfilled in you.

It may be no coincidence that a radical Puritan movement called the Grindletonians was active across the North of England in the first half of the seventeenth century, as this was also where Quakers developed in the early 1650s.

Quaker Beginnings: The Early Quaker Movement

The bitter disputes between mainstream and radical Puritans were temporarily set aside during the two English Civil Wars (1642–51), as both groups supported Oliver Cromwell and the Parliamentary cause against Charles I and the Royalists. In 1649, the execution of King Charles I led to the establishment of a Commonwealth under the rule of the Rump Parliament, and four years later Oliver Cromwell became head of state as the Lord Protector. During the English Commonwealth, mainstream Puritans gained political office, and the old conflicts re-emerged. Those in power viewed the radicals as heretics who threatened the social order. The radicals were angered by limited social and religious reform and demanded religious and political freedom. Puritans of all persuasions interpreted social conflict and turmoil as a sign of the coming end times and the imminent return of Christ. It was within this chaotic context that the Quaker movement emerged and became the most enduring offspring of radical Puritanism.[7]

George Fox (1624–91) was, arguably, the most important founder of the early Quaker movement. He was born into a Puritan family in Leicestershire, and as a young man, he began looking for a meaningful faith, traveling widely among the many radical religious groups that existed at the time. George had life-changing spiritual experiences which helped him form a coherent religious vision, and by the end of the 1640s, he was gathering communities of like-minded people in the Midlands and Yorkshire, including many gifted preachers who shared his convictions. This sense of mission was strengthened in 1652, when he had a vision at the top of Pendle Hill in Lancashire of "a great people to be gathered"; he then preached to a large group of spiritual seekers at Firbank Fell in what is now Cumbria. This drew other important figures into the movement and led to a momentous encounter with the Fell family, members of the local gentry living at Swarthmoor Hall, near Ulverston. Margaret Fell (1614–1702) and most of her household joined with Friends (Jn 15:14), having been convinced by the preaching of George Fox. Swarthmoor Hall then became the Quaker headquarters, and due to their political influence, the Fells were able to protect the embryonic movement. Margaret possessed a range of essential skills, including management, coordination, and political lobbying. She was also a gifted writer who provided spiritual counsel, promoted Quaker ideas, and defended the place of women in ministry. The other principal leader at this time was James Nayler (1618–60), a farmer from Yorkshire who had risen to the rank of Quartermaster in the Parliamentary Army. He was, perhaps, the most effective preacher and theologian of the first generation of Friends, whose charisma attracted fierce loyalty. In 1656 in Bristol,

James and his followers re-enacted Jesus's entry into Jerusalem as a prophetic sign, leading to a conviction for blasphemy, brutal public punishment, and imprisonment. It may be that his religious and political radicalism meant that he was viewed as a particular threat by those in power. Together, Fox, Fell, and Nayler formed a formidable team that could inspire and mobilize large numbers of people in pursuit of a common purpose. In 1654, having built a power base in the North, a large and well-organized team of Quaker ministers launched a huge preaching campaign all across the British Isles, Ireland, continental Europe, the Ottoman Empire, Palestine, the Caribbean, and the American colonies. In 1657, Mary Fisher and others managed to secure an audience with Sultan Mohammed IV in the Turkish city of Adrianople and were politely received. However, John Luffe and John Perrot, who traveled to Rome to speak with the Pope, were not so lucky. They were apprehended by the Inquisition and suffered torture. Luffe was executed, and Perrot spent three years in prison before returning to England. Similarly, Katherine Evans and Sarah Cheevers were held and interrogated by the Inquisition in Malta for nearly five years. This small English sect was beginning to have a global impact. Such success alarmed those in authority, and Fox met with Oliver Cromwell on multiple occasions, reassuring him that Friends posed no physical threat. This kind of diplomacy became a key aspect of Quaker strategy in subsequent years, but it was controversial. Some, like James Nayler, felt that their loyalty to God's kingdom left little or no room for compromise with the earthly authorities.

Why was the Quaker movement able to grow so rapidly and survive when other radical Puritan groups were short-lived? There are, perhaps, five key factors. The first Friends experienced a Pentecostal sense of spiritual empowerment that produced a fearlessly embodied witness. Apocalyptic expectations produced a fervent sense of urgency that invigorated their preaching mission. In addition, the movement was blessed with many gifted preachers and leaders who were capable of inspiring and mobilizing large numbers of people. The impact of these factors was magnified by the development of highly effective systems of organization. Finally, because the movement emerged initially in the North of England, its rapid growth took place out of view of those in power. By the time it became a visible threat, it was simply too strong and well-organized to be easily crushed. For a time, the Quaker movement looked as though it might turn the world "upside-down." However, with the fall of the Commonwealth and the Restoration of the monarchy in 1660, nonconforming religious groups faced harsh persecution, and Friends found themselves in a struggle for survival. This had a major impact on its subsequent development as a faith community, and this will be discussed in more detail in the next chapter.

Essential Features of the Early Quaker Movement

The spiritual vision of the first Friends represented a distinctively Christ-centered expression of the Christian faith. Because Friends believed that Jesus was now returning in Spirit to dwell within his people, they dispensed with any practice or belief that might distract them from a single-pointed focus on his inward presence. They felt they had rediscovered the faith that had been practiced by the earliest Church in response to Pentecost (Acts 2) and the creation of the new covenant (Hebrews 8).

Pentecost and New Covenant: A Universal Faith of Divine Intimacy

> Thus, is the living God purifying his Temples, and he is making a Glorious situation, a Heavenly Habitation, and an Everlasting dwelling place in the sons and daughters of men; for God is now come to dwell in his people.[8]

Through his Incarnation, Christ had established a new way of being human, a new covenant, and a new creation. In him, people were offered a transformed way of being human, fully in the divine image and likeness, an intimate inward relationship with God in Spirit, and the beginnings of a renewed creation in which God would be all and in all. Everyone could now benefit from this new opportunity, because the presence of Christ was universally and personally available through the Holy Spirit. At Pentecost, the apostle Peter proclaimed that God's promise, made through the prophet Joel, had been fulfilled:

> In the last days it will be, God declares, that I will pour out my Spirit upon all flesh, and your sons and your daughters shall prophesy, and your young men shall see visions, and your old men shall dream dreams. (Joel 2:28/Acts 2:17)

In addition, the author of the Letter to the Hebrews declared that God's promise, made through the prophet Jeremiah, to establish a new covenant of divine intimacy, had been fulfilled in Christ:

> This is the covenant that I will make with the house of Israel after those days, says the Lord: I will put my laws in their minds and write them on their hearts, and I will be their God, and they shall be my people. And they shall not teach one another or say to each other, "Know the Lord," for they shall all know me, from the least of them to the greatest. For I will be merciful toward their iniquities, and I will remember their sins no more. (Jer. 31:33-34/Heb. 8:10-12)

For Friends, in the new covenant, the spiritual presence of Christ replaced all the many physical and mediated ways people had used to connect with the divine in the old covenant. Therefore, their faith was characterized by an intimate inward relationship with God in Spirit, universally available, and unconstrained by human institutions, beliefs, and practices. Christians often assumed that they have replaced Jews as God's chosen people. However, Friends believed that, through the work of Christ, a covenant relationship had been offered to everyone. What had been outward, physical, mediated, and specific was now inward, spiritual, direct, and universal. This implied a fundamental shift in the divine–human relationship. It opened up membership of God's people to Gentiles as well as Jews; it transformed the outward law written on stone, into an inward law written in the heart; the bodies of all believers became the living temple of God; Christ, the eternal high priest, replaced human priesthood; and an experience of resting and feasting with Christ took the place of the outward Sabbath and holy days.[9] As God's people, Friends believed that they were ruled by Christ and would reveal his way of being human in their lives. He is the one in whom God and humanity, creator and creation, and heaven and earth meet. He is the eternal high priest, uniting his people with God, the eternal Prophet, teaching them divine wisdom, and the eternal king, ruling within them. Christ is gathering his scattered people. He is the head, and they are his body. All this led to a forceful rejection of what Friends regarded as corrupted forms of Christianity. They believed that, shortly after the apostolic period, the Church lost its dynamic sense of the inward rule of Christ and returned to the outward ways of the old covenant. They felt they were recovering the living faith of the earliest Church. Christ was appearing within his people,[10] and this was a sign that God was about to replace the kingdoms of the world with the kingdom of God. This faith appeared to herald the end of all forms of man-made religion and had radical implications for Quaker Spirituality.

The Inward and the Outward: A Contemplative and Charismatic Faith

One of the most distinctive features of the early Quaker movement was the way in which these Friends combined a quietist and contemplative form of worship and personal practice with a powerfully embodied and charismatic response. Their inward spiritual experiences were made manifest, both within the context of spirit-led worship and by the visible testimony of their lives in the world.

Communal Worship and Personal Practice

> Be still and cool in thy own mind and spirit from thy own thoughts, and then thou wilt feel the principle of God to turn thy mind to the Lord God, whereby thou wilt receive his strength and power from whence life comes.[11]

Because their understanding of the Christian faith was founded on an experience of becoming aware of God's presence and allowing the Holy Spirit to undertake its transformative work within people, for early Friends, both communal worship and individual spiritual practice needed to be based on a discipline of human surrender. To be yielded to God, it was necessary to stop all striving and become still, open, and attentive to the divine voice through a practice of "unprogrammed expectant waiting." This was unprogrammed in the sense that the community did not predetermine what would happen. Christ would order the worship himself. The task of the gathered people was to respond faithfully to his commands. This required discernment, the careful testing of spiritual leadings. It was called "expectant waiting," because the community gathered with a sense of excited anticipation about what God was about to do within them and through them. Although silent waiting was a well-established tradition within contemplative Christianity, for Friends, this practice produced a strongly embodied and charismatic response.

Human Transformation

> And by the fruits you bring forth you may know the tree, whether you be of the first birth or you be born again; and unless you be born again you cannot enter into the kingdom of heaven.[12]

Friends gave significant emphasis to spiritual transformation, believing that people could embody the divine nature in their lives through a three-stage process. The first stage was convincement, where the light revealed their spiritual deadness and alienation from God. The second stage was purification, an intense inward experience of cleansing and healing. The final stage involved entering a new life of divine indwelling and freedom from sin, bringing an overwhelming sense of joy and liberation. This was a born-again spirituality, in which Friends felt that they had died to the old, limited ways of Adam and had experienced new birth in the divine life of Christ. They felt it was necessary for people to participate in the birth, life, death, and resurrection of Jesus in their own inward experience. The way of Christ was the antithesis of the way of Adam. Life in Christ implied a dependence on the creator, an inward possession of God, and a life ruled by divine wisdom. Life in Adam, by contrast, meant a dependence on created things, an outward belief in a distant God, and a life ruled by limited human wisdom. The faith of Christ brought eternal life, whereas the faith of Adam led to death. Since God's perfection was revealed in Jesus, people could now share in this perfection as he came to dwell and rule within them. Although they remained physical creatures, the divine life was being channeled through them.

The Lived Faith: An Embodied Testimony

The experience of a life-changing inward encounter with God often prompted a strongly emotional and expressive physical response in the earliest Friends. Although worship began in silence and stillness, when the Holy Spirit moved among the gathered people, it was not uncommon for those present to exhibit charismatic behavior. This could involve physical shaking, ecstatic spirit-led utterance, and the urge to carry out dramatic signs conveying God's message to the world. Their opponents used lurid accounts of such conduct to portray Friends as outrageous and dangerous religious extremists; it seems that the label "Quaker" was initially applied to the movement as a term of abuse. Leading Friends felt compelled to justify their ways. In 1660, George Fox published *To All the Nations under the Whole Heavens*, defending Quaker behavior by highlighting the many biblical examples of people quaking and trembling when encountering the living God.[13] Friends responded to what they had encountered within worship in a number of visible ways: first, through a commitment to vigorous evangelism, in which itinerant ministers carried out forceful public preaching and publishing, achieving a global reach; and second, their physical lives gave a visible testimony to the way of Jesus in the world, reflecting his humility, truthfulness, nonviolence, and concern for the poor. This led them to reject the use of oaths (Mt. 5:33-37 and Jas 5:12) and to refuse to comply with accepted forms of social deference, such as the use of flattering titles or the removal of hats before social superiors (Acts 10:34 and Jas 2:1-4). In 1660, Friends publicly declared their peaceable principles to the recently crowned King Charles II:

> we certainly know, and testify to the world, that the Spirit of Christ, which leads us into all truth, will never move us to fight and war against any man with outward weapons, neither for the kingdom of Christ, nor for the kingdoms of this world.[14]

Early Quaker testimony also reflected Jesus's condemnation of spiritual hypocrisy and unjust religious authorities. They felt that the established Church in England was oppressive in its actions and impeded the true faith of inward divine intimacy. For them, the human priesthood, physical sacraments, and liturgies distracted people from the living presence of Christ and prevented them from enjoying the new life he offered. They condemned the wealth and power of the Church and resisted tithes as an unjust tax that financed the opulent lives of the clergy. The dominant religious culture seemed to be founded on professed belief, rather than on a living relationship with God and a transformed life. Most people were prepared to call God Lord but were unwilling to do what the Lord commanded (Lk. 6:46). For all these reasons, the testimony of early Friends seemed deeply threatening to those in power, provoking conflict and persecution. Harsh treatment at the hands of the authorities reinforced their identity as God's people, following in the footsteps of Christ.

Primitive Christianity Revived: A Distinctive Faith

> The sum and substance of true religion doth not stand in getting a notion of Christ's righteousness, but in feeling the power of endless life, receiving the power, and being changed by the power. And where Christ is, there is his righteousness.[15]

The experience of Friends as a Spirit-led people called to reveal the way of Christ within the world engendered a distinctive understanding of the true faith, which Friends believed represented the revival of primitive Christianity as it had been practiced in the first century. This had far-reaching implications for their understanding of key aspects of the Christian faith.

The Bible

Early Quakers distinguished between Christ the Word of God and the Bible, which was inspired by this Word. They argued that, since the living Word was the source of the Bible, it had to be the primary religious authority. However, the Bible was true and reliable when read under the guidance of the Spirit that inspired it.[16] Indeed, when approached in this way, people would hear God speaking through the text. These Friends read the Bible empathetically, placing themselves within the narrative and using it to interpret their own lives and experiences.[17] For example, writing to a William Osborne in 1657, Margaret Fell drew on chapter three of Luke's Gospel to encourage him to inwardly cut down any tree that did not bear good fruit and to make his internal paths straight to prepare the way for the Lord within him (Lk. 6:46). James Nayler used the parable of the prodigal son (Lk. 15:11-24) to highlight the distinction between a false faith focused on physical things and the true faith of inward divine intimacy. Nayler associated the former with the prodigal feeding on the pigs' husks, and the latter with the banquet organized by the son's father on his return to the family. He advised his readers that they should "not read this parable without knowing it, but within thee."[18] Feeling that they were living in the same Spirit as the prophets and the apostles, Friends identified with the dramatic biblical accounts of their exploits. Sometimes, this prompted them to carry out public signs as a form of prophetic drama, including going naked (Isaiah 20), and appearing in sack cloth and ashes (e.g., Neh. 9:1). The purpose of these signs was to shock people out of their complacency and provoke a spiritual crisis leading to repentance, so that they might turn to the guidance of God within them. Early Friends found that their distinct understanding of the new covenant was most powerfully expressed in the writings of the apostle Paul and the Gospel of John. They felt they were rediscovering the long-lost faith of the earliest Church. Unlike Reformed Puritans, early Friends did not regard the Bible as their only authority, and in some ways, their contemplative and empathetic approach to the Scriptures was more Catholic than Protestant.

The Church

Friends argued that it was the Holy Spirit, unconstrained by time, place, and culture, that gathered the true Church. What mattered was that people became aware of the Spirit's presence and were willing to submit to its guidance. Knowledge of the Bible and the stories of the historical Jesus were viewed as helpful but not absolutely essential. Robert Barclay described the Church as "no other thing but the society, gathering, or company of such as God hath called out of the world and worldly spirit, to walk in his Light and Life." So, its members were those who "are by the secret touches of this holy light in their souls enlivened and quickened, thereby secretly united to God."[19] Christ was the head of this Church, and the gathered people were his body. The rule of Christ was like the human brain, regulating the functions of the body's limbs and organs. The Church was a people gathered by the Spirit into union with God in the context of the unfolding end times.

The Ministry

Friends held a distinctive understanding of what it meant to be a minister. Every ministry, whether carried out as service or delivered as a divine message, was understood to be the work of Christ in Spirit acting in and through his people. It was not about being appointed to a particular position within a human institution; the initiative for ministry came from God, and the appropriate human response was to be attentive and faithful to the call.[20] Anyone might experience a call to ministry, regardless of social status, gender, age, education, or ethnicity. The role of the Church, as the gathered people of God, was to discern, identify, and recognize ministers within their community. Since all members of the body of Christ might receive a call to ministry, it has been suggested that early Friends not only affirmed the priesthood of all believers but effectively abolished the idea of a laity.

The Sacraments

Traditionally, the Church has defined a sacrament as an outward sign that conveys God's saving work within people. This has usually been associated with liturgical practices or ordinances, especially baptism and holy communion. The early Quaker understanding of the new covenant gave absolute priority to the inward presence of Christ in Spirit, so they saw no need for the physical celebration of the sacraments practiced by other churches. Indeed, these practices were regarded as a problem, diverting attention away from the immediate presence of Christ. It was the inward reality that mattered, whether this was baptism in the Holy Spirit or the inward experience of communion with God (Rev. 3:20). So, rather than rejecting the sacramental aspects of faith, early Friends internalized and universalized them. Any situation in which the spiritual presence of Christ is known and revealed in the lives of his people, individually and communally, is sacramental. What Friends have called testimony, Christ made known visibly in the embodied lives of believers, might be regarded as the primary Quaker sacrament.[21]

The Liturgical Year

Like many other groups emerging out of the Reformation, early Friends refused to follow the liturgical calendar of Church tradition. There were two main reasons for this. First, as Puritans, they associated the celebration of special times and seasons with the corruption of Christianity and the adoption of pagan practices. Second, because their faith focused on an ongoing participation in the work of Christ as an inward and spiritual experience, there seemed little value in memorializing past events, as God's saving and transforming actions were unfolding in the present. Every moment of every day holds the potential for a dynamic and life-changing experience of divine action.

The Creeds

For the first Friends, in the new covenant, becoming a member of God's people involved a transformative inward relationship with Christ in Spirit, rather than the profession of fixed statements of belief. Although these Friends seem to have accepted the essentials of Christian orthodoxy, they viewed creeds as inadequate and often misleading descriptions of the faith, which lacked the vibrancy of real divine encounter.

Turning the World Upside-Down: A Radical Faith

The radical nature of the Quaker way, as it was enacted during the 1650s, appeared to those in power to threaten the very basis of the existing social order. Their testimony seemed to undermine established social structures and challenged dominant understandings of the status of earthly government. In a culture where rigid social hierarchies were regarded as divinely ordained, Friends proclaimed that God did not recognize the validity of such human divisions (Acts 10:34). Some Friends proclaimed that, rather than being God's intention, inequality was a result of human sin in a fallen world. Those who demanded social deference from others were guilty of idolatry because only God is worthy of worship. In a deeply patriarchal society, where men confined women to the private sphere as personal possessions, Friends affirmed the public ministry of women living in the new covenant. In such circumstances, there was no longer male or female, for all were one in Christ Jesus (Gal. 3:28) and for men to stop a woman from speaking was to silence Christ speaking through her. The whole body of Christ, including men and women, should remain silent in the church (1 Cor. 14:34-35), because Christ is the bridegroom and the Church is his bride (Rev. 19:7). This experience of Christ living and speaking through them was powerfully liberating for early Quaker women, but their assertive public ministry was so transgressive of dominant social norms that it provoked real hostility. Deeply antagonistic attitudes to other cultures, races, and religions were common. However, early Quakers felt that such outward distinctions were merely temporary features of a fallen world. Human divisions were being overcome by the gathering of God's people in the Holy Spirit. This conviction seems to have enabled Friends to adopt a relatively enlightened attitude to people of other faiths, leading to several interesting encounters.[22] A fascinating consequence of this new spiritual vision was that it seemed to enable people to see the creation through divine eyes, rather than through a limited human perception. George Fox wrote that "all the creation gave unto me another smell than before, beyond what words can utter."[23] In Adam, humans are in a destructive relationship with the rest of creation, but in Christ, the right relationship is restored. People can understand the divine ordering of creation and become vessels through which God's love flows into the world. Finally, the Quaker experience of participating in a new humanity influenced their attitude toward government and the rule of law. Where Christ is the eternal king and ruler, the authority of earthly government inevitably becomes temporary and provisional. When people are ruled inwardly by Christ, and God's law is written on their hearts, earthly government is no longer needed to constrain them. At her trial in Lancaster in 1664, Margaret Fell declared, "I own allegiance to the King, as he is the King of England, but Christ Jesus is King of my conscience."[24]

The Early Quaker Vision: Key Points

In summary, in the early Quaker understanding of the true faith, all authentic knowledge of God comes directly by revelation rather than via human authorities or secondary sources. The Holy Spirit is universally available, enabling everyone to enjoy an intimate and inward relationship with God, where the divine law is written upon the heart and Christ teaches his people himself. Communal worship and personal spiritual practice are therefore rooted in a discipline of listening for and hearing God's voice and obeying the divine command. When people do this, they experience a spiritual death and resurrection, dying to the fallen way of Adam and being born again into the perfect way of Christ, so that their lives reveal the fruits of the Spirit—love, joy, peace, patience, kindness, generosity, faithfulness, gentleness, and self-control (Gal. 5:22-23). They are then gathered into a community of love and unity, which offers a glimpse of the kingdom of heaven on earth. However, this faith is regarded as foolish by the world, and so God's people tend to be vilified, misrepresented, and persecuted for their witness.

A Complex Legacy: The Roots of Quaker Diversity

The faith and practice of the first generation of Friends combined a complex mix of characteristics that presented future generations with a set of creative tensions to be negotiated and interpreted. Their spirituality was both contemplative and charismatic, their vision was both universalist and Christian, their witness was both opposed to the world and actively engaged with it, and their culture was both individualistic and communitarian.

The Quietist-Charismatic Tension

There was a creative tension in the early Quaker movement between a quietist and contemplative spiritual practice and a charismatic and emotionally expressive response. On the one hand, they emphasized the need for people to adopt an attitude of total passivity before God, surrendering the human will to the divine will. This led to a manner of worship focused on waiting in silence and stillness, allowing God, rather than humans, to order the service. Such a discipline looked a lot like the contemplative practices of medieval mystical piety. In 1661, Isaac Pennington offered a classic description of this discipline:

> Give over thine own willing, give over thy own running, give over thine own desiring to know or be anything and sink down to the seed which God sows in the heart, and let that grow in thee, and be in thee, and breathe in thee and act in thee; and thou shalt find by sweet experience that the Lord knows that and loves and owns that, and will lead it to the inheritance of Life, which is its portion.[25]

At the same time, Friends were called Quakers because of their powerfully embodied spirituality, and it has been suggested that the early movement was a forerunner of modern charismatic Christianity.[26] These Friends seem to have experienced a great sense of joy, fearlessness, and spiritual energy, revealed in physical shaking, ecstatic prophesying, dramatic signs, healings, and public preaching. Such a strongly embodied witness, particularly when enacted by women, transgressed accepted norms of human conduct and outraged polite society. As a result, their opponents condemned Friends for their religious enthusiasm, regarding them as a serious threat to social order.

The Universalist-Christian Tension

There was another creative tension within the early Quaker movement between spiritual universalism and Christian exclusivism. The first Friends believed that the Holy Spirit was unconstrained by place, time, and culture. What mattered was an awareness of the presence of Christ in Spirit and a willingness to submit to his transformative teaching. This was available to all people without exception. Such a view finds support in a number of passages within the New Testament (e.g., Acts 10:34-35 and Rom. 2:14) and was eloquently expressed by the eighteenth-century American Friend, John Woolman:

> There is a principle which is pure, placed in the human mind; which in different places and ages hath had different names. It is, however, pure, and proceeds from God. It is deep and inward, confined to no forms of religion nor excluded from any, where the heart stands in perfect sincerity. In whomsoever this takes root and grows, of what nation so ever, they become brethren in the best sense of the expression.[27]

On the other hand, these Friends were clear that Christ was "the way, and the truth, and the life" and the essential mediator between God and humanity (Jn 14:6). This suggests an element of Christian exclusivism, which was also reflected in their use of the Bible, their emphasis on liberation from sin and a life of holiness, and the centrality of being born again in Christ, through a life-changing personal conversion. For them, it was only possible for an individual to be in communion with God once they had been cleansed of sin. These aspects of the early Quaker movement are consistent with Evangelical Christianity.

The Separatist-Activist Tension

There was a third creative tension in the early Quaker movement between the need for separation from the corruptions of a fallen world and a desire to actively contribute to God's redemptive work within it. These early Friends regarded themselves as the one true Church and God's chosen people. They had been liberated from sin and evil and needed to protect themselves from its temptations and corruptions. Being in conflict with those around them resulted in persecution, and this seemed to validate their religious identity. In the Bible, they could see that God's people had always suffered at the hands of the world. This attitude is expressed clearly by Margaret Fell when she wrote to King Charles II in 1660:

> We who are the people of God called Quakers, who are hated and despised, and everywhere spoken against, as people not fit to live, as they were that went before us, who were of the same spirit, power, and life.[28]

Despite this caution about the world, the power and energy of the early Quaker movement was driven by apocalyptic urgency, a sense that God was acting in their time to overturn all earthly kingdoms and establish the kingdom of God. This led them into the world as spiritual combatants in the Lamb's War, encouraging all people to turn inwardly to God and sharing the good news they had experienced themselves. In the words of James Nayler, these Friends were committed to showing "love to the lost" and being "a hand held forth to the helpless to lead out of the dark."[29] So, despite their concerns about the corrupting ways of the world, they were willing to actively engage with other people, religious groups, and social institutions in the name of God's saving work. For this reason, while they tried to maintain a state of spiritual independence, they did not seek to be physically separated from the world.

The Individualist-Communitarian Tension

Finally, there was a creative tension in the early Quaker movement between the individualism implied by a belief that all people could enjoy an intimate inward relationship with God in Spirit and the conviction that Christ was gathering his scattered people into a new cohesive spiritual unity. They believed that Christ had come to teach his people himself, and he would speak directly to them without the need for human mediators or authorities. In rejecting what they perceived to be the corruptions of other churches, the first Friends tended to prioritize the immediacy of personal experience over systems of organization or belief. At the same time, their sense of spiritual regeneration suggested that their separate personal identities had been transcended, as Christ came to dwell and rule within them. The apostle Paul's words seemed to express this well, "it is no longer I who live, but it is Christ who lives in me" (Gal. 2:20). The Church was both a single body and an interconnected set of limbs and organs, in which every element had value and a part to play. At the same time, these limbs and organs had no meaningful existence apart from the whole body and the ordering power of its head (1 Cor. 12:12-26). As the Quaker movement developed and grew, Friends had to find a way to balance their rejection of man-made institutions with their identity as a gathered and ordered people.

In the mid-seventeenth century, the Quaker movement established an alternative vision of the Christian faith which was distinctive, coherent, and unified. However, across history, this vision has developed, changed, and diversified.

Notes

1. Purchasing indulgences was a way to reduce the amount of punishment one had to undergo for sins.
2. Salvation as the work of God alone is called monergism, as opposed to synergism, where God and humanity cooperate in the process.
3. Anabaptist-rooted churches include the Mennonites, the Amish, the Hutterites, and the Church of the Brethren.
4. For an overview of Anabaptist spirituality, see C. Arnold Snyder, *Following in the Footsteps of Christ: The Anabaptist Tradition* (London: Darton, Longman & Todd, 2004).
5. See David Como, *Blown by the Spirit: Puritanism and the Emergence of an Antinomian Underground in Pre-Civil-War England* (Redwood City, CA: Stanford University Press, 2004).
6. Nigel Smith, *Perfection Proclaimed: Language and Literature in English Radical Religion, 1640-1669* (Oxford: Clarendon, 1989), 2.
7. For the history of Quaker beginnings, see Rosemary Moore, *The Light in their Consciences: Early Quakers in Britain, 1646-1666* (University Park, PA: Pennsylvania State University Press, 2000).
8. Dorothy White, *A Visitation of Heavenly Love* (1660).
9. Catherine M. Wilcox, *Theology and Women's Ministry in Seventeenth Century English Quakerism: Handmaidens of the Lord* (Lampeter: Edwin Mellen Press, 1995), 36–7.
10. This has been called the "apocalypse (i.e., revelation) of the Word," Douglas Gwyn, *Apocalypse of the Word: The Life and Message of George Fox, 1624-1691* (Richmond, IN: Friends United Press, 1986).
11. George Fox and John L. Nickalls, eds., *Journal* (London: Quaker Home Service, 1997), 346.

12 James Nayler and Licia Kuenning, eds., *The Works of James Nayler*, Volume 1 (Glenside, PA: Quaker Heritage Press, 2003), 52.

13 George Fox, *The Works of George Fox*, Volume 4, Doctrinal Books I (New York: AMS Press, 1975), 255–8.

14 *A Declaration from the Harmless and Innocent People of God, called Quakers* (1660). The whole declaration is available online, http://www.qhpress.org/quakerpages/qwhp/dec1660.htm.

15 Isaac Pennington, "Letters to the Friend of Francis Fines," in Britain Yearly Meeting, *Quaker Faith and Practice* (Britain Yearly Meeting, 1994), 19.30.

16 Robert Barclay, *Apology for the True Christian Divinity* (Glenside, PA: Quaker Heritage Press, 2002), 62–84.

17 See Michael L. Birkel, *Engaging Scripture: Reading the Bible with Early Friends* (Richmond, IN: Friends United Press, 2005).

18 Nayler, *The Works*, Volume 1, 159.

19 Barclay, *Apology*, 231–2.

20 Terry H. Wallace, et al., *Traditional Quaker Christianity* (Barnesville, OH: Ohio Yearly Meeting, 2014), 91–4.

21 Paul Anderson, *Following Jesus: The Heart of Faith and Practice* (Newberg, OR: Barclay Press, 2013), 117–19.

22 See, for example, Justin J. Meggitt, *Early Quakers and Islam: Slavery, Apocalyptic and Christian-Muslim Encounters in the Seventeenth Century* (Uppsala: Swedish Science Press, 2013).

23 Fox, *Journal*, 27.

24 Isabel Ross, *Margaret Fell: Mother of Quakerism* (York: William Sessions, 1984), 172.

25 Isaac Pennington, *Some Directions to the Panting Soul* (1661), in Britain Yearly Meeting, *Quaker Faith and Practice*, 26.70.

26 Paul Alexander, "Historical and Theological Origins of Assemblies of God Pacifism," *Quaker Theology* 12 (2005/6), https://quakertheology.org/assemblies-of-god-pacifism/ (1 May 2025).

27 John Woolman, and Phillips P. Moulton, eds., *The Journal and Major Essays of John Woolman* (Richmond, IN: Friends United Press, 1989), 236.
28 Terry S. Wallace, *A Sincere and Constant Love: An Introduction to the Work of Margaret Fell* (Richmond, IN: Friends United Press, 1992), 49.
29 Nayler, *The Works,* Volume 3, 47.

2

The Branches

Quaker Diversity

This chapter traces the development of the Quaker movement from the late seventeenth century to the present time and examines the factors that caused divisions and separations within it, which led to a complex and diverse global family of Friends in the world today.

The Restoration Period: A Struggle for Survival

The Context

During the 1650s, the embryonic Quaker movement, filled with the Holy Spirit, was on the offensive, fearlessly proclaiming the good news that Christ was returning in Spirit, offering everyone an intimate inward relationship with God, and establishing God's Kingdom on earth. Friends felt that they were fighting in the final and decisive spiritual battle against the power of evil that had polluted humanity and corrupted the rest of creation. However, the death of Oliver Cromwell in 1658 acted as the catalyst for a chain of events leading to the collapse of the Commonwealth and the Restoration of the monarchy in 1660. Before returning to England, Charles II promised to uphold religious toleration. However, the new Cavalier Parliament sought to restore the old order with the Church of England as the only legitimate church in the country, and the Act of Uniformity in 1662 effectively outlawed the worship of all nonconforming religious groups. Because of their rapid growth and visible public profile, Friends were regarded as a particular threat, and the Quaker Act of 1662 required them to swear an oath of allegiance to the king, contrary to their religious convictions. As a result, the years that followed were traumatic and costly. Some eleven thousand Friends were imprisoned during the reign of Charles II, and as many as four hundred and fifty died, including most of the movement's original leadership, largely due to insanitary jail conditions. Instead of fighting the Lamb's War, Friends found themselves struggling for survival.

The Response

Faced with such a perilous situation, Friends drew on their well-developed organizational skills to achieve three key objectives: to become a highly disciplined and well-ordered people who could withstand persecution; to mount an effective political lobbying campaign for religious toleration; and to manage their public image and reassure the authorities that they were no physical threat to the social order. During the next twenty years, the Quaker community transformed itself from a dynamic Spirit-led movement led by charismatic leaders into an increasingly centralized and regulated body with an organizational hierarchy of meetings and a method of decision-making designed to enable God to rule through the community in an ordered way. Quakers became conversant with the law, using this knowledge to contest persecution. Legal advice was made available, sufferings were meticulously recorded, and there was systematic lobbying of Parliament. Prominent Friends, such as George Fox, recognized that, to achieve toleration, the movement needed to convince those in power that Quakers were a harmless and law-abiding people. This objective was pursued in several ways. Written declarations were issued to those in power affirming the peaceable principles of Friends. Publishing in the name of Quakers became tightly controlled, and any threatening warnings or questionable doctrines were censored. The Quaker movement was evolving into an alternative community.[1]

The Implications

While Friends were willing to face imprisonment and death in defense of their religious convictions, other aspects of the earliest movement were regarded as dispensable if they undermined the primary objectives of survival and toleration. This had a significant impact on the evolution of Quaker ways.

Quaker Social Witness

One of the main reasons early Quakers alarmed those in power was that they appeared to threaten established social hierarchies and institutions. Like the apostle Paul, these Friends proclaimed that there was no longer Jew or Gentile, slave or free, or male or female, for all were one in Christ (Gal. 3:28). This seemed to undermine accepted distinctions between people based on ethnicity, social status, and gender, reflecting the radicalism of the English Revolution. However, Friends' primary concerns were spiritual rather than political. In the context of persecution, they emphasized inward spiritual liberation, separated from any social or political demands. Spiritual equality did not necessarily mean social equality. The sight of assertive women preaching in public was viewed as scandalous, and while Quakers maintained their commitment to the ministry of women, in other ways their freedom became more curtailed, and their efforts were directed toward more acceptably feminine concerns. In the 1650s, James Nayler had condemned social inequality as the fruit of human sinfulness,[2] but by 1678, Robert Barclay argued that such distinctions were not contrary to God's intentions:

we say not hereby that no man may use the creation more or less than another. For we know that, as it hath pleased God to dispense it diversely, giving to some more, and some less, so they may use it accordingly.³

The issue of enslavement provides a good illustration of this shifting position. As some Friends became involved in the slave-based economy of the British Empire, especially in Barbados and the American colonies, George Fox did not feel able to condemn the practice. Instead, drawing on biblical sources, he advocated a practice of enslavement which softened some of its harsher aspects. Enslaved people, for example, were to be included in the Quaker family and its worship.⁴

Quaker Spiritual Practice

A similar dynamic shaped the development of Quaker spirituality, as the inward and quietist aspects of early Quaker practice began to take precedence over more animated and charismatic expression. The spiritual fervor of the first generation had been denounced as religious extremism and viewed as particularly objectionable when revealed in women's bodies. As a result, the movement increasingly discouraged public displays of charismatic behavior and threatening messages directed at those in power. The spiritual fire of a movement's pioneers often dies down in the second generation. Instead of forging something new, people inherit a pre-established set of traditions. The embodied sense of Christ coming to dwell within his people was replaced by a spirituality that focused on quietly attending to inward divine guidance.

The "Keithian Controversy": A Sign of Things to Come

Conflict among early Quakers tended to emerge around issues of religious authority, because, if everyone has Christ as their inward teacher, how could one individual or group tell others what to do?

This prompted Friends to give greater emphasis to the communal testing of individual leadings. In the 1690s, however, the movement experienced its first serious doctrinal dispute. Scottish Friend, George Keith, who was working in the American colonies, became uneasy about the lack of doctrinal awareness among Friends. He felt the belief that the inward Light was entirely sufficient for salvation seemed to devalue the importance of the atoning work of the historical Jesus. In pursuing his concerns, he provoked conflict with Quakers in America and England and was eventually excluded by both ("disownment"). At this time, Friends found unity in a common identity and culture, rather than in shared belief. Keith wanted greater clarity and consistency of belief, while his opponents preferred flexibility and ambiguity.[5] Although he found himself on the losing side, the issues Keith raised did not go away. By the early nineteenth century, many Friends had become more comfortable with orthodox Christian doctrine. This set the scene for subsequent separations within the Quaker community and the development of Quaker diversity.

Restoration Quaker Profiles

William Penn (1644–1718) became a significant Quaker leader in the late seventeenth century, using his social connections to lobby on behalf of Friends. Charles II granted Penn the American colony of Pennsylvania in payment of a debt owed to his father, where Penn attempted to create a place of religious toleration known as the "Holy Experiment." Penn's writings on matters of theology and politics had an influence on the development of the United States. Notable Scottish Friend, Robert Barclay (1648–90), was the most important theological writer of the Friends' second generation. His *Apology* defended the orthodoxy of Quaker belief while distinguishing it from Reformed Calvinism. He supported George Fox on a mission to continental Europe and was the nominal governor of the American colony of East Jersey.

The "Quietist" Period: A Peculiar People

The period of Quaker history sometimes called "Quietist" stretched from the 1690s to the 1820s. Friends increasingly distinguished themselves from the wider society and were viewed as a peculiar people. Religious enthusiasm declined as the charismatic aspects of the past largely disappeared, and a spirituality of quiet inwardness became dominant. At the same time, it also saw the expansion of Quaker communities within the American colonies and the increased involvement of Friends in politics, trade, industry, and science. Many Friends gained substantial wealth through investment in the slave-based economy of the British Empire, even though, by the end of the period, Quakers as a community had become committed abolitionists. This was a transatlantic Quaker world characterized by unity and diversity. Four general trends can be identified: a spiritual separation from the world, existing in parallel with increased practical engagement with it; an intense focus on communal discipline as the basis of unity and a marker of the true church; strictly regulated behavior existing alongside a generous approach to acceptable belief; and the emergence toward the end of the period of substantial doctrinal differences that eventually undermined Quaker unity.[6]

A Peculiar People

The impact of the struggle to survive within a hostile world, and the related need to manage internal conflict, prompted a growing emphasis on order and uniformity within the Quaker community. It was this that began to shape the public image of Friends as a peculiar people. The establishment of effective governance structures and shared discipline and testimony maintained group cohesion. This was most visible in the development of Quaker plainness. Friends always felt that their behavior should reflect loyalty to Christ and the guidance of the Holy Spirit, even if this made them seem peculiar to others. Acts of social deference, flattering speech, frivolous activities, and vanity in matters of dress implied worship of the human creature rather than God. As a result, Friends committed themselves to moderation in the use of material possessions and the avoidance of displays of vanity. They also practiced plain speech, refusing to accept the dominant rules of civility that required a person of higher social status to be referred to as "you." Instead, they used the more common terms of "thee" and "thou" for everyone. During the Quietist period, these practices were increasingly standardized and enforced as a way of protecting the purity of the true Church within a fallen world. Although this meant that behavior was highly regulated, it seems that acceptable belief was defined much more generously. However, in the latter part of the period, disputes over belief began to undermine unity, leading to conflict and schism. This reflected increasing tensions between distinct quietist, rationalist, and evangelical theological tendencies among Friends, which led to separations during the nineteenth century.

As the Quaker community grew and became dispersed, Friends needed to find ways to sustain unity and cohesion. Traveling ministers, epistles, and publications were all used to maintain connections between the scattered network of Quaker communities. While London and Philadelphia became the two principal centers of Quakerism during this period, new areas of settlement also began to develop. While a common discipline bound these groups together, a variety of local expressions emerged over time. The Quaker approach to marriage also reinforced cohesion through the application of endogamy, where Friends were only able to marry other members of their faith community. This was another important aspect of Quaker peculiarity.[7]

Engagement with the World

During this period, Friends defined themselves as a peculiar people (Tit. 2:14), spiritually separated from the world, but they also interacted with the wider society and managed their relationship with it. In some cases, this involved a positive engagement with worldly activities. This brought wealth and respectability but also presented significant challenges and potential compromises. Such an accommodation with the surrounding culture meant that Friends accepted established social hierarchies. This may have made it easier for them to justify their lucrative involvement in a slave-based economy and, within the colonies, to gain land and wealth at the expense of Indigenous Americans. At the same time, Quakers found that their spiritual values and ethics could both support and hamper their success in business, and their nonconformist ways often led to negative public portrayals. Success in worldly affairs sat uncomfortably with the Quaker discipline, with its emphasis on plainness. A distinction developed between those known as "Plain Friends," who rigorously observed the discipline, and "Gay Friends," who did not. However, in the mid-eighteenth century, a spiritual reformation took place. This produced a more rigorous enforcement of the discipline and a greater concern for social ethics, including the communal commitment to the abolition of enslavement. It also led to an increase in disownment, reducing the size of the Quaker community. For example, between 1750 and 1790, Philadelphia Yearly Meeting disowned 50 percent of its birthright members.

Quietist Quaker Spirituality

After the Restoration of the Monarchy, Friends retained their quiet and contemplative ways but began to play down the more charismatic aspects of the earliest years. In the Quietist period, this trend continued and intensified. The ways of inwardness and passivity gained preeminence. This reflected the Quaker conviction that the human will should be surrendered to the divine will and that this was best achieved by waiting on the Lord in silence and separating oneself from the corruptions of the world. Inspired by this heritage, Quietist Friends on both sides of the Atlantic felt that the best way to approach God was through a contemplative prayer of inward silence, where human thoughts and feelings were subdued. They lacked the spiritual assurance and conviction of the pioneering generation, and this led to greater caution about trusting spiritual experiences and motivations. Patient waiting and careful discernment came to constrain physical expression and action. Human motivations were treated with suspicion, and the virtues of humility and patience were emphasized. Worship became quieter as this sense of spiritual caution reduced spoken messages, which Friends call vocal ministry. The importance of applying careful discernment before speaking is reflected in the words of the eighteenth-century Quaker minister Susanna Morris:

> I think we are never safe unless we feel the plough of God's power and the hammer thereof so operating in us as to break us into tenderness, then it is that we know how to demean ourselves before him who can and does work such a change that any of his ministers are truly made able to speak.[8]

Three additional key themes can be identified within the evolving Quietist spiritual mindset: that achieving a perfectly reconciled relationship with God was a gradual life-long process, rather than a sudden and unexpected event; that obedience to the inward Light of Christ was sufficient for salvation, and so not entirely dependent on knowledge of the Bible or the historical Jesus; and that holiness was associated more with the discipline of the community than with individual piety. In view of this Quietist spiritual orientation, Friends during this period have often been characterized as inward-looking, passive, and world-denying. However, they were actively involved in the wider society, particularly within the economic sphere. Throughout the period, and especially during the mid-eighteenth-century Quaker reformation, Quietist spiritual practice prompted a concern for social justice and reform. A new generation of younger Friends, in seeking to enforce Quaker discipline in the face of growing conformity to the ways of the world, began to reconnect the Quaker community with the social radicalism of its founding mothers and fathers.[9]

Quietist Quaker Profiles

John Woolman (1720–72) spent most of his life in New Jersey. He is best known for his antislavery witness among Friends, but he also had active concerns for Native American rights, nonviolence, economic justice, and ecology. Woolman's spirituality, combining Quietist surrender with a dynamic commitment to social action, helped inspire the Quaker reformation in the mid-eighteenth century. His *Journal* is regarded as one of the most important Quaker spiritual autobiographies. Philadelphian teacher and writer Anthony Benezet (1713–84) was descended from a French Huguenot family. He was active in the areas of abolitionism, Native American rights, temperance, peace, and education. While Woolman concentrated his efforts within the Quaker community, Benezet addressed the wider world. His writings on enslavement helped inform the development of the abolitionist movement and were quoted by the Methodist leader, John Wesley.

The Nineteenth Century: A Divided People

During their first two centuries, Friends were largely successful in maintaining unity through the enforcement of a common discipline which regulated conduct, while allowing flexibility of belief. However, in the early nineteenth century, the fault lines between competing theological positions began to grow, influenced by wider social and religious factors. The Enlightenment, with its emphasis on human reason, inspired developments in philosophy and science that challenged traditional religious beliefs. At the same time, the Methodist revival movement gave birth to evangelicalism, which stressed biblical authority, the need for conversion, and works of piety and mercy. This situation posed a challenge to Quietist Quaker ways, and growing numbers of Friends began identifying themselves as evangelicals.[10] In the resulting conflicts, by 1860, a once-united American Quaker community had split into three distinct branches.[11] British and Irish Friends, while experiencing similar tensions, managed to avoid any major schism.[12] The names of three important nineteenth-century Quaker ministers are associated with each of the three divergent branches: Elias Hicks, with an ultra-Quietism which eventually moved toward modern rationalism;[13] Joseph John Gurney, with orthodox evangelicalism; and John Wilbur, with orthodox Quietism. Despite these upheavals, the social engagement of Friends constituted an area of continuity, with continued success in business, increasing wealth, and significant involvement in philanthropy and social reform activities.

Quaker Profiles: Nineteenth-Century Schisms

An American preacher from Long Island, New York, Elias Hicks (1748–1830), traveled widely in the ministry. His spirituality was rooted in eighteenth-century Quietism, at a time when many Friends were moving in an evangelical direction. His emphasis on spiritual experience over fixed doctrine and an allegorical approach to the Bible brought him into conflict with Friends who were more sympathetic to orthodox Christianity. John Wilbur (1774–1856) was also a preacher and traveling minister from Long Island. Although broadly orthodox, he defended traditional Quaker ways in the face of growing evangelicalism. This included balancing the authority of the Holy Spirit and the Bible, and a preference for Quietist waiting worship over a more active and expressive faith. Born into an English banking family, Joseph John Gurney (1788–1847) mixed banking work with a scholarly approach to Bible study, church history, and science. Influenced by the revival movements, Gurney argued that traditional Quaker ways and understandings were entirely compatible with evangelical Christianity. This brought him into conflict with Wilbur and his followers while traveling in the ministry in America.

The Two Great Separations

Two significant schisms undermined the unity of the North American Quaker community. In both cases, the essential point of disagreement was the relationship of Quakers to Protestant Christianity. Were Friends the one true Church that revived primitive Christianity, or were they a particular expression of Protestantism? Linked to this were disagreements about the extent to which Friends should collaborate with other churches.[14]

The Hicksite-Orthodox Separation

The Methodist movement has exercised a powerful influence on Quakers since its emergence in Britain during the late 1730s. Many Friends felt an affinity with the Methodist faith in its emphasis on the transformative power of the Holy Spirit, the universal availability of salvation, and the possibility of inward and outward holiness. However, some aspects of Methodism differed significantly from traditional Quakerism: it was founded on Scriptural authority; asserted the separation of justification and sanctification;[15] accepted a forensic understanding of atonement;[16] and valued emotionally expressive programmed worship, including the physical sacraments of water baptism and holy communion. As a growing number of Friends warmed to evangelical theology, these differences proved troubling to those committed to protecting Quaker peculiarities. In the 1820s, Elias Hicks represented those Friends worried about the increasing influence of evangelicalism, which they viewed as man-made and worldly. Orthodox Friends tended to be more evangelical and willing to engage with others. Those who supported Hicks were more likely to be suspicious of the world. Orthodox Friends felt that Quietist Friends undervalued the historical Jesus and placed too much emphasis on the Inward Light to the neglect of the Bible. They were committed to the essentials of Christian orthodoxy. For his part, Hicks wanted to uphold the Quietist view that the Light was sufficient for salvation, with the Bible being a secondary authority. He understood atonement to be an inward participation in the work of Christ, rather than a legal transaction. He also questioned more literal understandings of the Bible, preferring more metaphorical interpretations. To his opponents, this seemed like a dangerous departure from orthodox Christianity. In this conflict and the resulting schism of 1827, the London Yearly Meeting, which had come under the influence of evangelicalism, supported Orthodox Friends. Initially, Hicksites were Quietists who regarded the Orthodox as dangerous innovators, but many soon began to move in a liberal direction. This led to tensions between traditionalists, who were opposed to involvement in worldly affairs, and reformists, who wanted to work with others on social and political concerns. A new generation of young Hicksites identified as religious progressives, supporting freedom of thought and biblical criticism, opposing substitutionary atonement, and rejecting the idea of eternal punishment for sin. This shift toward a more liberal position led to a decline in plainness and increased cooperation with non-Quakers in the public sphere. In this way, Hicksite Friends became precursors of modern Liberal Quakerism.

Quaker Profiles: Hicksite Quaker Women

Born in Nantucket, Massachusetts, Lucretia Mott (1793–1880) was one of the most influential Quaker women ministers in nineteenth-century America. She combined a deep spirituality with an active social witness in several areas, including abolitionism, women's suffrage, Native American rights, temperance, penal reform, and peacebuilding. Her approach to faith and social justice has inspired Friends across the divides. Susan B. Anthony (1820–1906) was an American women's rights activist who lived most of her life in Rochester, New York. She balanced her family business with her political activism. Anthony collaborated with Elizabeth Cady Stanton, forming the American Equal Rights Association. She was an effective public speaker who traveled widely in support of women's suffrage, becoming president of the National Women's Suffrage Association in 1892.

The Wilburite–Gurneyite Separation

By the 1840s, a similar tension existed among Orthodox Friends, in this case between Quietists and Evangelicals. Joseph John Gurney exemplified the kind of evangelicalism that became dominant within Orthodox Quakerism, and by the mid-nineteenth century, most Orthodox Friends felt comfortable within the Evangelical culture that surrounded them. In contrast to this, John Wilbur and his supporters represented the Quietism of the past. This conflict produced a second series of separations during the 1840s and 1850s. However, more would follow later in the century, as the impact of Evangelical Revivalism began to be felt on Quaker worship practice and ministry. Again, although these conflicts existed among British and Irish Friends, where the evangelical tendency was dominant, they did not result in any serious long-term schism.

Evangelical Friends regarded Scripture as their principal authority and felt that the experience of the Inward Light, when separated from the Bible, could easily lead people into delusions. Gurney used the metaphor of the sun and the moon: the Bible was like the sun, being the essential source of light, whereas the Inward Light was like the moon, merely a reflection of that source. In terms of salvation, these Friends followed the standard Reformed position, which saw justification and sanctification as a two-stage process. People were saved by faith in the atoning work of Jesus and would only then receive the Holy Spirit, leading to sanctification. When it came to worship, Evangelicals viewed Quietist Quaker meetings as spiritually barren, lacking a vibrant sense of divine encounter, with infrequent vocal ministry. They preferred a more active approach to the spiritual life. An increased identification with other Evangelical Christians prompted them to soften traditional Quaker peculiarities. They ended the practice of endogamy, relaxed the requirements of plainness, and focused more on religious education and the need to nurture effective preaching. This expression of the Quaker faith combined the distinctive vision of Friends with mainstream Evangelical theology. Gurney was an Evangelical, but he retained a Quaker commitment to unprogrammed waiting worship, the rejection of outward sacraments, and the experience of inward spiritual guidance. Subsequently, as the evangelical influence intensified, all these commitments would be questioned.

The Wilburites, on the other hand, were traditionalists who wished to remain faithful to the ways of past generations of Friends. This animated their opposition to evangelicalism, which, in turn, led to separation. They upheld Barclay's view that the living Word of God was the fountain of divine revelation, and the Bible was merely a declaration of this fountain. They felt that Gurney's teachings gave too much emphasis to Scripture, at the expense of the active presence of God. In their view, this undermined the significance of the Inward Christ and neglected the living faith in favor of orthodox belief. Rather than being a discrete two-stage event, they continued to see salvation as an inward participation in the death and resurrection of Jesus, in which justification and sanctification represented a single ongoing process. Being Quietists, they upheld unprogrammed waiting worship, visible Quaker peculiarities, and the need for a spiritual hedge protecting them from a corrupting world. These Friends were also opposed to what they regarded as the excessive emotionalism of evangelical worship.

The Quaker Community at the End of the Nineteenth Century

During the last three decades of the nineteenth century, three significant factors set the scene for the development of Quakerism throughout the twentieth century: the impact of Wesleyan Holiness Revivalism; the beginnings of global evangelical Quaker missions; and the emergence of Liberal Friends.

Revivalism and the Pastoral System

From the late 1860s, many North American Evangelical Friends came under the influence of the Holiness Revival movement, with its stress on the importance of a second blessing of entire sanctification and the use of large-scale camp meetings. The success of this movement brought large numbers of new converts to Friends and coincided with the spread of the Quaker community through western migration. Such significant growth prompted major changes in practice. In responding to this geographical expansion and numerical growth, Evangelical Friends began to adopt what has been called the Pastoral System, which involved a more programmed form of worship, like other Protestant churches, and the appointment of pastors to take responsibility for preaching, teaching, and the coordination of worship services. By 1900, all but one American Evangelical yearly meeting (Baltimore) had embraced the Pastoral System. These developments created further tensions among Friends. Some, who were unhappy with the Pastoral System, formed Conservative meetings, finding common ground with Wilburite Friends. The more moderate evangelicals resisted calls to tolerate water baptism and holy communion and tried to find a balance between traditional Quaker distinctives and revivalist innovations. A conference of Gurneyite Friends in Indiana held in 1887 resulted in the Richmond Declaration of Faith.[17] While this was in many ways an orthodox Protestant statement of faith, it also drew a line in the sand, clarifying how far Quakers were prepared to go in an Evangelical direction without ceasing to be Friends. Those Evangelical Quakers who continued to draw inspiration from the holiness revival movement formed the Evangelical Friends Church. Until the late nineteenth century, the Quaker community had been concentrated in Britain, Ireland, and North America. However, one enduring legacy of the Evangelical influence on Friends at this time was the development of missions to other parts of the world. This work produced significant numerical growth and the creation of a genuinely global family of Friends. Quaker missions have been particularly successful in East Africa and in Central and South America.

The Beginnings of Liberal Quakerism

While many Evangelical Friends were being inspired by the Holiness Revival, some Gurneyites began to move in a different direction, influenced by Liberal Protestant theology. These Friends welcomed progressive developments in science and biblical scholarship, and this undermined their evangelicalism. Both Evangelicals and Liberals felt that Quietist Quaker peculiarities limited community growth and hampered cooperation with other Christians. As a result, the protective spiritual hedge began to be cut down. Although British and Irish Quakers had been influenced by the Evangelical movement, this did not lead to the kinds of changes to worship practice and ministry witnessed in parts of North America. A conference of British Friends held in Manchester in 1895 became a watershed moment, where modernist thought and liberal theology replaced Evangelicalism. Instead of causing schism, this led to the transformation of British Quakerism as a whole.[18] In America, similar changes enabled some Hicksite and modernist Gurneyite yearly meetings to reunite, helping to form modern Liberal Quakerism.

The Twentieth Century: A Diverse Global People

Although the twentieth century saw some successes in reconciling yearly meetings that had previously separated, the major developments during this period served to further fragment the Quaker community. On the one hand, Evangelical Friends witnessed substantial growth through the success of their global missions. On the other hand, a Liberal expression of the Quaker way developed, which rejected Evangelicalism and, over time, became increasingly pluralist and post-Christian.

Global Evangelical Missions

The extraordinary success of Evangelical missions produced a genuinely global Quaker community on an unprecedented scale. The first mission to Kenya in 1902 marked the beginning of this major global expansion. Across the century and into the new millennium, this missionary work was undertaken by two distinct groups of Friends: Friends United Meeting, a broad-based orthodox body accommodating diversity on matters of doctrine and practice, and the Evangelical Friends Church International, an alliance of Evangelical Friends with roots in the Holiness Revivals. Because these two groups have tended to avoid duplication, their church-planting activities have produced new communities of Friends in many different locations. There are now over two hundred thousand Friends in Africa, concentrated in Kenya, Uganda, and Burundi. This accounts for more than half of all Quakers in the world. Significant growth has also been achieved in Central and South America, with around seventy thousand Friends, mainly in Bolivia and Guatemala. This means that over 90 percent of Quakers in the world today are Evangelical, with pastors and programmed worship. The three countries with the largest number of Friends are Kenya, the United States, and Bolivia.

As Quaker communities in the Global South continue to grow, while those in Europe and North America experience decline, the future of the Quaker movement will be increasingly shaped by developments in the majority world. These Friends tend to be more socially and theologically conservative compared to their Western counterparts. They are less materialistic, more charismatic, and have a greater focus on the end times and on the existence of heaven and hell after death. It is not surprising, therefore, that these Friends are troubled by what they perceive to be the spiritual coolness and materialism of Western Quakers and by what they regard as a toleration of unbiblical practices in the areas of marriage and sexuality.[19] This may lead to reverse mission, where ministers from previously colonized settings seek to reinvigorate the spiritual life of Western Quaker communities who had previously evangelized them. The emerging faith and practice of Friends in the Global South, shaped by a range of different social and religious contexts, is producing fresh expressions of Quaker spirituality. For example, the significant presence of Pentecostalism within Africa and Central and South America is making its mark on worship practices, prompting a recovery of the more charismatic dimensions of the early Quaker movement, which have been neglected elsewhere.

East African Quaker Profiles

Daudi Lung'aho (1872–1967) was one of the first Africans to join the American missionary work in Kenya. Along with his wife, Maria Maraga (1873–1956), he was an important early leader and evangelist within East Africa and a supporter of the equality of men and women before God. Rasoah Mutua (1895–1996) was one of the first women to train as a Quaker pastor in Africa. She served on the board of East Africa Yearly Meeting and was an advocate for women, especially through her ministry in women's prisons. Maria Atiamuga (1903–81) was a significant Quaker minister in Kenya who focused her preaching on the needs of women's meetings. She was a key figure in the development of Women's Yearly Meeting in 1951 and served as deputy presiding clerk of East Africa Yearly Meeting (1957–60).

Liberal Friends

During the nineteenth century, many Friends were influenced by Methodist and Anglican evangelical theology. By the twentieth century, however, a new generation of Friends were finding inspiration from these same sources, but this time, in the form of liberal theology. The impact of Liberal Protestant theology on these Friends can be seen in five principal areas: (1) an acceptance of modern developments in science, including the theory of evolution; (2) a willingness to view the Bible as a text to be interpreted within its historical context; (3) an appeal to human reason and experience as the basis of religious authority; (4) a focus on the man Jesus as a model to follow; and (5) an optimistic view of human nature and the general trajectory of history. These themes acted as a counterpoint to the Evangelical emphasis on the Scriptures, human sinfulness, the need for Christ's atoning sacrifice, and a vision of the afterlife based on heaven and hell. An engagement with Liberal theology also prompted a recovery of those aspects of the early Quaker vision neglected by Evangelicals.[20]

This included an emphasis on spiritual experience over doctrine and Scripture and on the work of the Holy Spirit in the here and now over the atoning work of the historical Jesus. Liberals accused Evangelicals of neglecting the writings of early Friends and sought to rectify this by undertaking new research into Quaker history.

Liberal Friends pointed to the importance of continuing revelation within the Quaker tradition and interpreted this revelation in a progressive way, where truth is revealed more fully over time. They noted the significance of divine indwelling for early Friends, and universalized it, arguing that all of life could be sacramental. This was quite different from the first generation, who asserted a radical separation between God's people and the fallen world. Rather than denouncing music and the arts as frivolous and ungodly, they were willing to see God's presence within them and potentially in all areas of life. Quakerism was reconceived as an expression of mysticism, in which life-changing spiritual experiences were available to all. The open and experiential nature of mysticism seemed to fit well with the modern liberal mindset. Finally, a commitment to equality led to changes in Quaker ways. Liberal Friends ended the practice of formally recording ministers who are discerned to have a special gift of service to offer the community and arranged the seating for worship in circles or squares, rather than in rows facing a raised bench for elders and recorded ministers. Overall, these Friends combined traditional Quaker practices with modern Liberal theology and removed whatever was left of the spiritual hedge that separated Friends from the rest of society.

Liberal Quaker Profiles

A member of the York family of confectioners, John Wilhelm Rowntree (1868–1905), was a leading figure in the development of Liberal Quakerism. In addition to being a traveling speaker, he helped establish the Summer Schools movement and the Woodbrooke settlement in Birmingham to promote new thinking and the application of modern biblical scholarship and science to the Quaker faith. He also initiated a major project producing a set of up-to-date volumes on Quaker history. When Rowntree died young, Rufus Jones (1863–1948) continued his work, characterizing Quaker spirituality as communal mysticism with a universalist potential and a strong commitment to peace and social justice. While this made him the most significant Liberal Quaker thinker in the twentieth century, he also attempted to reunify some Quaker communities divided by earlier schisms.

Pluralist Liberal Friends

The prominence Liberal Friends have given to spiritual experience, separated from any external source of religious authority, has enabled a Pluralist form of Quakerism to emerge that is both theologically diverse and increasingly post-Christian. Rather than shared belief, what holds Pluralist Liberal Friends together is a preference for silent unprogrammed worship, the freedom of individuals to follow their own spiritual journeys, and support for a Liberal social and political interpretation of Quaker testimony. This means that Pluralist Liberal Quaker culture tends to be permissive in terms of belief, gender identity, and sexual ethics. Because spiritual experience is beyond simple rational formulation, claims to truth can only ever be partial and personal. As such, Pluralist Liberal Friends subscribe to the "absolute perhaps," meaning that the only thing they can be certain about is that they can never be absolutely certain.[21] They value the journey, but have no particular interest in reaching a destination. This attitude is reflected in their books of discipline, which are less doctrinally prescriptive than those of Orthodox Friends and tend to focus on writings representing a diversity of spiritual experience and interpretation. Pluralist Quaker communities have become safe spaces for those whose sexual orientation and gender identity is fluid or nonconforming. Demographically, however, they remain overwhelmingly white and relatively affluent.

Quaker Universalists

The pluralist tendency among Liberal Friends accelerated during the final years of the twentieth century, producing a form of religious universalism which mirrored the multicultural and multi-faith character of many Western societies. This perspective is reflected in the following statement from the Quaker Universalist Group:

> Spiritual Awareness is accessible to everyone of any religion or none, and no one person and no one faith has the final revelation or monopoly of truth. Such awareness may be expressed in many different ways. We delight in this diversity.[22]

Universalist Friends feel that the Quaker way provides a flexible framework within which individuals can follow their own spiritual path, drawing on a range of religious and secular sources of inspiration. This expression of Quakerism takes religious pluralism for granted and makes it an essential feature of the community, enabling the phenomenon of "hyphenated Quakers" to emerge. These are Friends who have dual religious affiliations. Sometimes this involves engagement with another Christian denomination, but it might also mean a commitment to the practices of some other faith tradition. Buddhism, Neo-Paganism, and other new spiritualities are popular among some Pluralist Liberal Friends. In a positive sense, the pluralism of modern Liberal Quakerism implies a recognition of the value of all faiths and encourages respectful dialogue. However, it also presents challenges. Experimenting with another faith tradition can easily slip into cultural appropriation, so sensitivity is required. The desire to engage with other faiths may lead, unintentionally, to practices that disrespect them. Pluralism can also downplay uniqueness in favor of the universal, which may seem disrespectful to those who value the distinctiveness of their faith tradition.[23]

Quaker Nontheists

Quaker nontheism represents another distinctive expression of Pluralist Liberal Quaker culture, reflecting growing skepticism within Western societies about traditional understandings of God.[24] Nontheism is diverse in nature, but finds unity in a rejection of realist conceptions of the divine, especially when these see God as a creator and supreme ruler. Instead, God is understood by humanist nontheists to be a social construction reflecting human values and ideals. Beliefs about God are viewed as stories that communicate important truths. British Quaker nontheist, David Boulton, explains that, "being Godless for God's sake is about taking leave of an idol for the sake of the values and the truth that the idol has been held to represent."[25] Despite their nonrealism, what seems to attract nontheists to Friends is their appreciation of the shared disciplines of worship and decision-making, the value of being part of a supportive community, and the ethical life that is implied by the general orientation of Quaker testimony.

Quakers in the New Millennium

At the beginning of the new millennium, three main groupings of Friends can be identified: Conservative, Pastoral-Evangelical, and Liberal. Despite their differences, each group finds its roots in the vision of the earliest Friends. In the last chapter, four creative tensions were identified within the early Quaker movement: the quietist-charismatic, the universalist-Christian, the separatist-activist, and the individualist-communitarian. None of the current Quaker groupings reflect all the characteristics visible in the first generation, as each tends to emphasize some and downplay others.

Conservative Friends

Conservative Friends are a small grouping who seek to maintain traditional Quaker peculiarities. This means that they uphold a quietist and contemplative form of worship and spirituality, rather than being charismatic and emotionally expressive. While they are explicitly Christian, their faith has a universalist dimension, due to the emphasis given to the Living Word, available to everyone. These Friends remain cautious about involvement in the world and are therefore more separatist than activist. They also tend to give greater priority to communalism than individualism.

Pastoral and Evangelical Friends

Pastoral and Evangelical Friends are a large and diverse grouping who tend to be divided into two general tendencies: those who are more modernist in orientation and those who have been influenced by Holiness Revivalism. They are more likely to have an emotionally expressive spirituality than other Quakers. Having moved closer to an orthodox Protestant position, these Friends tend to be suspicious of universalism. Modernists are more likely to be involved in social activism than Holiness Evangelicals, who have a greater focus on saving souls. Both seek to achieve a balance between the individualist and the communitarian, in which the need for individual conversion and salvation is set alongside the importance of being part of the wider Christian Church.

Liberal Friends

Liberal Friends are a relatively small grouping who are divided into two main tendencies: Liberal Christians, and post-Christian and nontheist Pluralists. They both value a more contemplative, unprogrammed form of worship, in which charismatic and emotional expression is not encouraged. Both are sympathetic to universalism, but Pluralists regard this as an essential aspect of their Quaker identity. Liberal Friends of all sorts see no need to separate themselves from the world and often work with other like-minded people on social and political concerns. Liberal Quaker culture tends to be more individualistic than communitarian.

Despite their many differences, all the diverse expressions of the Quaker way that exist in the world today trace their roots back to the distinctive vision of the earliest Friends, and this has produced a spirituality and practice which has a coherent shape and orientation.

Notes

1 For a comprehensive history of Restoration Quakerism, see Richard C. Allen, and Rosemary Moore, eds., *The Quakers, 1656–1723: The Evolution of an Alternative Community* (University Park, PA: Pennsylvania State University Press, 2018).
2 Nayler, The *Works*, Volume 1, 66–7.
3 Barclay, *Apology*, 433.
4 Hilary Hinds, *George Fox and Early Quaker Culture* (Manchester: Manchester University Press, 2011), 141–5.
5 Madeleine Ward, *The Christian Quaker: George Keith and the Keithian Controversy* (Leiden: Brill, 2019).
6 For a wide-ranging exploration of the "Quietist" period, see Robynne Rogers Healey, ed., *Quakerism in the Atlantic World, 1690–1830* (University Park, PA: Pennsylvania State University Press, 2021).
7 The use of the term "peculiar" points to the way the distinctive behavior and appearance of Friends distinguished them very clearly from those around them in the wider society.
8 Margaret Hope Bacon, *Wilt Thou Go on My Errand? Three 18th Century Journals of Quaker Women Ministers* (Wallingford, PA: Pendle Hill Publications, 1994), 64.

9 Nikki Coffey Tousley, "Sin, Convincement, Purity, and Perfection," in *The Oxford Handbook of Quaker Studies*, ed. Stephen W. Angell and Pink Dandelion (Oxford: Oxford University Press, 2013), 179.

10 Thomas D. Hamm, "Hicksite, Orthodox, and Evangelical Quakerism, 1805–1887," in Angell and Dandelion, *The Oxford Handbook of Quaker Studies,*, 63.

11 Thomas Hamm, and Isaac Barnes May, "Conflict and Transformation, 1808–1920," in *The Cambridge Companion to Quakerism*, ed. Stephen W. Angell and Pink Dandelion (Cambridge: Cambridge University Press, 2018), 31.

12 For a detailed exploration of these significant changes, see Stephen W. Angell, Pink Dandelion, and David Harrington Watt, eds., *The Creation of Modern Quaker Diversity, 1830–1937* (University Park, PA: The Pennsylvania State University Press, 2023).

13 Hick himself was an ultra-Quietist, but his emphasis on the sufficiency of the Inward Light began a process that led Hicksite Friends in a modern rationalist direction.

14 For more information on these significant changes, see Thomas D. Hamm, *The Transformation of American Quakerism: Orthodox Friends, 1800–1907* (Bloomington, IN: Indiana University Press, 1988).

15 Justification means being regarded as righteous by God, whereas sanctification involves being cleansed of sin.

16 In the forensic understanding of atonement, Jesus's death is understood as punishment for human sin, required to satisfy divine law.

17 The Richmond Declaration of Faith is available online: http://www.quakerinfo.com/rdf.shtml.

18 For a thorough analysis of this process, see Thomas C. Kennedy, *British Quakerism, 1860–1920: The Transformation of a Religious Community* (Oxford: Oxford University Press, 2001).

19 Arthur O. Roberts, "Evangelical Quakers, 1887–2010," in Angell and Dandelion, *The Oxford Handbook of Quaker Studies*, 123–4.

20 Rhiannon Grant, *Hearing the Light: The Core of Quaker Theology* (Alresford, Hants: Christian Alternative Books, 2021).

21 Pink Dandelion, *An Introduction to Quakerism* (Cambridge: Cambridge University Press, 2007), 244.
22 The Quaker Universalist Group: https://qug.org.uk/.
23 Mark Russ, *Quaker-Shaped Christianity: How the Jesus Story and the Quaker Way Fit Together* (Winchester: Christian Alternative Books, 2022), 23–4.
24 Dan Christy Randazzo, "Quakers and Non-theism," in Angell and Dandelion, *The Cambridge Companion to Quakerism*, 274.
25 David Boulton, ed., *Godless for God's Sake: Nontheism in Contemporary Quakerism* (Dent: Dales Historical Monographs, 2006), 6.

Part Two

Spirituality and Practice

3

The Inward

Quaker Worship and Spiritual Practice

Introduction

This chapter explores the meaning of communal worship and personal spiritual practice within the Quaker tradition. What is distinctive about the worship and spiritual practices of Friends, how did these take shape within the early Quaker movement, and how have they changed over time? Before this, however, let's just consider what worship means in a more general sense. The root of the word worship in Old English is *worðscip*, which means to have "worth-ship," to be worthy of reverence. Humans worship whatever they believe has the greatest worth in their lives. They give their attention to whatever is valued the most. So, if a "god" is defined as whatever people value the most and pay the greatest attention to, there are many gods within human culture. This might include things such as wealth, power, reputation, and celebrity. Organized religions, especially those within the Abrahamic tradition, tend to distinguish between the worship of false gods and the worship of the one true God. In this context, idolatry is defined as the worship of something which is not, by its nature, the one true God. Worship has been defined as a "service of praise, adoration, thanksgiving, and petition directed toward God through actions and attitudes."[1] Within a Christian context, this service is focused on the saving actions of God within human history, with a particular emphasis on Jesus Christ, where God is understood in Trinitarian terms as Father, Son, and Holy Spirit. For example, in worship, praise is directed to God the Father, through Jesus Christ the Son, by the power of the Holy Spirit. It is often assumed that worship is demanded by God. However, it may simply be a natural and appropriate human response to who God is, what God has done, and what it is hoped God will do in the end. It is not so much that God requires praise and adoration, but that humans need worship, as it defines their identity and gives direction to their lives.

The dominant forms of Christian worship across history are rooted in three distinct practices, visible within the earliest Church.[2] These communities adopted a simple form of ritual based on the Last Supper; a communal approach to reading and interpreting the Scriptures together; and a Spirit-led practice of waiting upon the Lord. The first of these practices developed into liturgical worship focused on the Eucharist, in which ritual is used to encourage an awareness of God's presence and draw people into the divine life and its mysteries. Here, the worshipper's attention is focused on the priest and the altar. This was the predominant form of Christian worship from about the fourth century until the Protestant Reformation in the sixteenth century and is characteristic of the "high churches," particularly in Eastern Orthodoxy and Roman Catholicism. The second form of worship, based on reading and preaching on the Scriptures, with less fixed ritual, has become the accepted practice among the "low church" traditions of Reformed Protestants. The primary purpose of this worship is to remember and give thanks for God's saving actions recorded in the Bible. In this case, the worshipper's attention is focused on the preacher and the pulpit. The third worship practice largely dispenses with formality and ritual in favor of a more fluid and spontaneous response to the divine presence. This approach is most evident today among the various modern charismatic churches that have come to dominate global Christianity. In this case, instead of priest and altar, or preacher and pulpit, the worshipper's attention is focused on an inward spiritual experience and an embodied outward charismatic response.

The discussion below explores the emergence of a distinctive form of worship among early Friends in the seventeenth century, considers how it was formalized by subsequent generations, and traces the way Quaker worship practice has diversified since the nineteenth century. In terms of the three general models of worship noted above—the formal liturgical, the semiformal preaching, and the informal charismatic—Quaker practice has tended to give priority to the Spirit-led and spontaneous. However, all three styles are present in quite distinct ways.

Traditional Quaker Spirituality

Unprogrammed Waiting Worship

As already noted, the Quaker way was founded on an experience of God's powerful inward presence and the capacity of the Holy Spirit to teach and transform people. The purpose of both communal worship and individual spiritual practice, therefore, was to make people aware of this presence and attentive to divine guidance. Friends found that the best way to do this was a practice of unprogrammed waiting worship, in which the community sat together in silence and stillness to listen and attend to the divine presence. This was unprogrammed because what might occur was not planned, and it involved waiting as people paused their normal thoughts and activities and waited for God to act.

Early Quaker Worship

In the religious and political turmoil of early modern England, the practice of waiting on the Lord in silence appears to have had two very different meanings. Some spiritual seekers who searched in vain for the true Church began to wait in silence as an act of despondency. However, during the English Revolution there was a growing sense of excitement that Christ would soon return to establish his kingdom on earth. For some, this prompted a pentecostal experience of the outpouring of the Holy Spirit, and people began to gather in silence, waiting in eager anticipation for signs of God's coming reign. What had previously been a practice of waiting in despondency became an experience of waiting in hopeful expectancy. Accordingly, the earliest Quaker form of worship is best understood as an end-times practice. Its primary focus was on God's saving actions as they were unfolding in the present, rather than on the remembrance of things past. So, this worship was profoundly shaped by a powerful sense of being caught up in the transformation of all things. As Christ began to appear in Spirit within his people, the physical rule of the earthly powers was being replaced by the spiritual rule of God. Worshippers felt that the long-awaited unveiling of God's new creation was finally taking place. This generated a strongly embodied response, including physical shaking and quaking, ecstatic prophetic utterance, dramatic public signs, healings, and other miracles.

Descriptions and Metaphors

Quaker worship, during its apocalyptic phase, seems to closely reflect the events surrounding the beginning of the Church at Pentecost (Acts 2:1-21) and the practices of charismatic Christians in the world today. In each of these situations, there appears to be a close connection between the worship experience and a sense of being caught up in the end times. The apostle Paul offers a description of worship that seems to reflect this unprogrammed and Spirit-led method:

> When you come together, each one has a hymn, a lesson, a revelation, a tongue, or an interpretation. Let all things be done for

building up. If anyone speaks in a tongue, let there be only two or at most three and each in turn, and let one interpret. But if there is no one to interpret, let them be silent in church and speak to themselves and to God. Let two or three prophets speak, and let the others weigh what is said. If someone sitting receives a revelation, let the first person be silent. For you can all prophesy one by one, so that all may learn and all be encouraged. (1 Cor. 14:26-31)

In 1659, the early Quaker minister, Edward Burrough, described the way this style of worship was experienced in the earliest Quaker movement:

> While waiting upon the Lord in silence, as often we did for many hours together, with our minds and hearts toward him, being stayed in the light of Christ within us from all thoughts, fleshly motions and desires, we received often the pouring down of the spirit upon us, and our hearts were made glad and our tongues loosened, and our mouths opened, and we spake with new tongues, as the Lord gave us utterance, and his spirit led us, which was poured upon sons and daughters.[3]

Another early Quaker minister, Francis Howgill, observed how the practice of waiting on the Lord generated an intense sense of spiritual intimacy and community cohesion:

> The Kingdom of Heaven did gather us and catch us all, as in a net, and his heavenly power at one time drew many hundreds to land. We came to know a place to stand in and what to wait in; and the Lord appeared daily to us, to our astonishment, amazement and great admiration, insomuch that we often said one unto another with great joy of heart: 'What, is the Kingdom of God come to be with men?'[4]

A good biblical metaphor reflecting apocalyptic Quaker spirituality is Jesus's teaching in the Gospel of Luke about the need for watchfulness (Lk. 12:35-38). He cautions his followers to "be dressed for action and have your lamps lit" (v. 35), which implies adopting a disposition of spiritual attentiveness and discernment, being ready to see, hear, and feel the inward action of the Holy Spirit. The worshippers are "like those waiting for their master to return from the wedding banquet" (v. 36): they need to be ready. Christ will come to dwell within his people, who are a temple of living stones. The worshippers must be prepared to "open the door for him as soon as he comes and knocks" (v. 36). God does not act coercively, but rather by invitation, so people need to be ready to answer this call, which could come at any time, day or night. The practice of attentiveness and watchfulness, therefore, is essential both in worship and during the normal activities of daily life.

Traditional Unprogrammed Worship

The essential shape of unprogrammed waiting worship has been sustained across Quaker history and is still practiced by Conservative and Liberal Quakers today. However, the sense of being caught up in the end times soon waned, and greater emphasis was given to being faithful in the "meantime," patiently awaiting the fulfillment of God's saving actions. Christ the Eternal High Priest is understood to be present among the worshippers and it is he, rather than any human authority, who orders the worship. The gathered people sit and wait, giving their attention to God in a state of inward and outward stillness and silence. As a temple of living stones and a holy priesthood, God comes to dwell among them and within them. As a living sacrifice, they surrender their human wills in favor of the eternal divine will (1 Pet. 2:5). This understanding of worship has, perhaps, been most closely maintained within Conservative Quaker communities, as this passage from the *Book of Discipline* of Ohio Yearly Meeting (Conservative) demonstrates:

> In our assemblies the Holy Spirit speaks directly to the human soul, and worship is a personal communion with God and a yielding of our wills to the Divine will, for which no form or aid of clergy is

necessary. This communion may be realized in a true and vital way though there be no vocal service. A living silence may be so filled with the Divine Presence that all who worship become conscious of it and are drawn together in unity under the power of His love.[5]

Such a sense of divine intimacy also reflects the metaphors of Christ as the true vine and as the head of a body with many limbs and organs. In worship, the gathered people abide in their living connection with him. He is the true vine, and they are the branches. If they allow it, the divine life can flow through him and into them, as it rises from the roots (Jn 15:1-5). Here is a form of Holy Communion in which the worshippers are nourished by God as an inward and spiritual experience. They are also like a physical body, where Christ is the head and the assembled group are the many organs and limbs. In worship, the head guides and directs the body. Every person has an essential role because the body can only function when all its parts are working together. In this way, Christ, the head, and the body of his people come together as a unity in diversity, where the whole is more than the sum of its parts (1 Cor. 12:12-31). It has been suggested that this type of worship has a closer affinity with High Church liturgical forms than with Protestant practice. While Protestants tend to focus their worship on the reading of Scripture and a sermon, traditional Quaker and liturgical worship is centered on the real Presence of Christ. Friends, however, have internalized and spiritualized this liturgy, giving priority to what they understand to be the inward spiritual substance over the outward physical sign.[6] A distinct Eucharistic experience of Holy Communion is to be found in the silence, deep within the hearts of the gathered worshippers:

> The silent worship of a Quaker meeting is communion insofar as it rises above silence as a symbol and allows the life of God into the souls of the waiting group. The worshipper becomes a part of the divine life, as it flows through, and transforms.[7]

In unprogrammed worship, the worshippers must be still so that they can be attentive to the divine presence. This enables God to become active, ruling in human hearts. Within this form of worship, an individual may feel a divine call to give a message to the gathered people. This is an example of divine utterance or prophecy, which Friends have tended to call vocal ministry. Although responsibility for the worship and spiritual life of a Quaker community is shared by all its members, some Friends exercise particular care of these things as Elders and Recorded Ministers.

Elders

Elders are given special responsibility for nurturing the spiritual vitality of the community and for ensuring that worship is conducted in good order. They seek to support the spiritual development of individuals, encourage opportunities for teaching and learning, and promote helpful vocal ministry within worship.

Recorded Ministers

Some Friends are recognized as having gifts in the areas of vocal ministry, preaching, and teaching. When this is discerned by a community, those individuals will be encouraged to exercise these gifts and may be formally recorded as ministers. Recorded ministers often visit communities to provide spiritual inspiration or to raise awareness of a particular concern.

Types of Meeting for Worship

In traditional Quaker spirituality, unprogrammed waiting worship is at the very heart of the communal life of Friends. It is a discipline that is used for several different purposes, including the normal weekly meeting for worship, weddings, funerals, and business meetings. Worship meetings for conducting church business are considered in more detail in the next chapter.

Metaphors for Unprogrammed Waiting Worship

Playing in a Spiritual Orchestra

In traditional Quaker spirituality, the discipline of waiting on the Lord is the same for both individual spiritual practice and worship. However, communally, the experience can be quite different. British Friend, Beatrix Saxon Snell, noted that "those who persevere in group worship know that it differs from private devotion as the music of an orchestra differs from the music of a single player."[8] This orchestral metaphor is helpful in describing the nature and experience of unprogrammed waiting worship. Christ is the conductor, each person is an individual instrument, and the gathered people are the orchestra.[9] The Holy Spirit is like the music channeled through the assembled players. As worshippers, Friends must accept that they are not in control. They haven't composed the music and aren't conducting the orchestra. Nevertheless, if people pay close attention to the conductor and the score, the music will come to life through them. In this way, the transforming love and wisdom of God flows through the gathered people just as music flows through an orchestra. Music has the capacity to inspire us, provoking a powerful emotional response, but it can also be unpredictable. Sometimes, the playing of the orchestra blends seamlessly in harmony, producing music of indescribable beauty, a genuinely uplifting heavenly sound. On other occasions, things might not work so well. There may be a lack of cohesion and coordination among the players, the experience feels awkward, and the music seems discordant and jarring, lacking a sense of magic and grandeur. Understandably, the performers savor those extraordinary times when the music has real vitality, full of exuberance and intensity, but they must also accept that sometimes it will be dull, uninspiring, and run-of-the-mill. This does not mean that the individual players should give up and disband the orchestra. It means that everyone must exercise patience, keep practicing, and live with the hope that the vitality will return. Each musician contributes to this by practicing their own instrument regularly and keeping it tuned and in good condition.

The Doctor's Waiting Room

Quaker worship might also be compared to a group of people sitting in a room, waiting to be called to see a doctor or surgeon. The Spirit is like a divine physician, whose work within identifies the sickness, prescribes the remedy, and restores the patient to health. The Light shines within us like an X-ray, revealing what is wrong. Like a doctor, divine judgment diagnoses the condition and recommends the treatment required. The Spirit's sanctifying power, like a surgeon, takes invasive action, putting right what has gone wrong. Finally, divine love and compassion, like a nurse, care for the patient throughout the process. Are people prepared to listen to the doctor's advice, or will they harden their hearts, ignore the symptoms, avoid the diagnosis, and try to run away from the problem? If they are willing to consult the doctor of their souls and trust in the expertise of the divine surgeon, they may be nursed back to spiritual health.

Traditional Spiritual Practices

Quaker spirituality is focused on nurturing an intimate and transformative inward relationship with God in Spirit. Friends have therefore adopted spiritual practices that help them to cultivate a deepening sense of the divine presence and to weave this into all aspects of their lives. Every important long-term relationship requires ongoing care and attention, and one's communion with God is no exception. To be serious about this practice requires it to become a daily discipline rather than merely a weekly event. If God is truly present, an experience of holy communion is always available. If there is a stumbling block, it may simply be due to a lack of conscious awareness. Friends have found that giving regular attention to their inward lives and developing a capacity to be still and receptive enables them to enter more deeply into communal worship. People need to become both *broken and tender*.[10] If there is a barrier, hindering their relationship with God, how can it be removed so that they can become more spiritually receptive? To function within a harsh world, people tend to protect themselves emotionally by forming a tough shell. However, to experience the divine presence, this shell needs to be softened and broken open. Being broken means becoming open and available, so that the Spirit is free to do its work and the Light can reveal what was previously hidden. This is about preparing the ground of the inward garden, tilling the hard soil, so that the divine seed can begin to grow there. Tenderness is also important. Sensitivity to touch acts as a metaphor for spiritual receptiveness. Tenderness means feeling things more intensely. A numbness gives way to enhanced spiritual sentience, helping Friends to notice the divine presence and what God is doing within them. This is not necessarily a comfortable experience, as it requires a practice of surrender, a lowering of defenses, and a certain vulnerability. This can be painful and traumatic, but Friends have found that it is the gateway to new life. Here are three specific methods that Friends have found helpful in becoming broken and tender: practicing quiet waiting and contemplative prayer; setting aside times of retirement; and reading devotional writing.

Quiet Waiting and Contemplative Prayer

Early Friends were suspicious of set techniques or routines in the inward life, preferring a more spontaneous and flexible approach. Their letters of spiritual guidance encouraged people to stop, turn inward, and wait on the Lord in a spirit of surrender and attentiveness, but they rarely specified methods of achieving this. Over time, Friends became more willing to adopt practices drawn from other contemplative Christian traditions. For example, in her book about personal spiritual practices, Patricia Loring highlights the use of contemplative methods drawn from Catholic spirituality.[11] In order to attend to the divine presence, Friends have sometimes used a prayer of inward silence similar to practices within Carmelite spirituality.[12] By stilling the body and mind, Friends have found it possible to experience an increased awareness of God's presence, leading to an enhanced perception of the nature and order of things. This involves learning the "language of silence" through a discipline of deep listening.[13] Given the Quaker view that all times and places can be sacramental, it is perhaps not surprising that the ceaseless prayer recommended by the apostle Paul (1 Thess. 5:17) has found a place within Quaker spirituality. Twentieth-century American Friend Thomas Kelly advocated such a practice. By using a short, repeated phrase, Friends might carry an inward stillness with them wherever they go and in whatever they are doing. This is like the use of the Jesus Prayer within the Eastern Orthodox tradition. Kelly offered the following guidance:

> Walk on the streets and chat with your friends. But every moment behind the scenes be in prayer, offering yourselves in continuous obedience. . . . If you slip or stumble, and forget God for an hour, and assert your old proud self, and rely on your own clever wisdom, don't spend too much time in anguished regrets and self-accusations but begin again, just where you are.[14]

Times of Retirement

The Quaker commitment to sustaining an inward awareness of the divine presence can easily be frustrated by the distractions and demands of daily life. In responding to this challenge, Friends have taken times of solitude or "retirement," during which they remove themselves from all outward concerns and activities to attend exclusively to the inward life. This might mean going on a retreat for an extended period, but it could equally involve setting aside one day each week, or perhaps an hour every day for this purpose. Such a practice is often encouraged in advices and queries, for example:

> Do I make a place in my daily life for inward retirement and communion with the Divine Spirit? To what extent has this brought satisfaction spiritually? Are there ways in which I might attain greater satisfaction or inspiration? Does my daily schedule need review and revision at this time?[15]

Although the discipline of taking times of retirement is not enforced in a prescriptive way, it may require lifestyle changes, such as adjustments to daily routines. The eighteenth-century American Quaker John Woolman resolved to scale back his business activities so that he could dedicate more time to his inward spiritual life and his outward social concerns.[16]

Devotional Writings

Friends have found a variety of devotional writings helpful in nurturing their spiritual lives. Although these are no substitute for direct inward communion with God, they can be a valuable source of encouragement and inspiration that provide guidance and reveal how the Spirit has worked in the lives of others. When read empathetically, the Scriptures have provided Friends with a treasured window through which to view the inward spiritual life. Robert Barclay suggested that the Bible is like a mirror, reflecting people's own circumstances, challenges, and dilemmas described in the lives and actions of the biblical characters.[17] Because the Scriptures were inspired by the same Spirit that dwells within people today, they still have the capacity to illuminate one's inward spiritual experiences. In a similar way, Friends have found great benefit in reading the spiritual journals of those who have gone before them. Journaling is a long and well-established practice among Friends, and, like the Bible, such writings offer insights into the way God was active in the lives of those recognized for their spiritual discernment and faithfulness. Finally, epistles of spiritual counsel have been important across Quaker history. These have tended to be modeled on the New Testament epistles, which Friends have valued for the wisdom they impart. Such letters are not primarily about establishing doctrine, but rather about the need to build up and nurture the community through encouragement, admonishment, and spiritual guidance.[18]

Metaphors for Quaker Spiritual Practice

Waiting: Advent and Holy Saturday

Although traditionally Friends have not observed the Christian liturgical calendar, they hope to experience it inwardly as a spiritual participation in the birth, life, death, and resurrection of Jesus. So, for example, Advent and Holy Saturday may serve as meaningful metaphors for the discipline of individual and communal waiting. Advent is a period of waiting and deep reflection in preparation for Christmas, a time for remembering the birth of Jesus, and anticipating his second coming. Holy Saturday represents another period of quiet and somber reflection following Good Friday, a time to mourn the death of Jesus and wait for his resurrection. When Friends intentionally stop what they are doing, become quiet and still, and pay careful attention to the Holy Spirit within them, they are adopting an Advent practice, waiting in hopeful anticipation for Christ to be born within them. Similarly, they are also participating in Holy Saturday, waiting with expectancy and longing for Christ to be resurrected within them. Having experienced this spiritual birth and resurrection, Christ comes to dwell within them, as inward teacher, healer, priest, counselor, liberator, and king.

Tuning In: The Transmitter and the Antenna

In modern telecommunications systems, transmitters turn electrical signals into radio waves. These send out words, pictures, and other information that can travel great distances. To receive these radio waves, an antenna or aerial is required to act as a receiver for the passing information. An antenna is a metal rod or dish that takes the radio waves and turns them into electrical signals, which can be used by a radio, television, or telephone system. However, to work effectively, an antenna needs to be carefully tuned into the radio waves sent by the transmitter. It must be set up properly, located in the right place, and pointed in the right direction. If this is not done, the signals are available, but they may not be received. This offers another helpful metaphor for the purpose of spiritual practice. In Quaker spirituality, the problem is not God's absence, but rather an inability to perceive this presence and receive divine communication and guidance. God is constantly reaching out like a transmitter. However, the antenna may not work if it has not been set up properly. It could be disconnected or pointing in the wrong direction. Receipt of a clear signal requires a practice of quiet attentiveness, waiting, and listening, of seeking to tune one's spiritual antenna to the divine transmitter. Taking times of retirement and using devotional writings can act as antenna tuners, helping to optimize the capacity of the inward receiver to connect with the heavenly transmitter. In this way, a previously blank screen may suddenly be filled with vivid sounds and images.

Being Still: Muddy Water Becomes Clear

When standing water is disturbed, it is cloudy and opaque, as sediment gets stirred up and mixed with the water. When this happens, it is difficult to get a clear view. There may be fish or interesting plants in the pond, but they may not be visible. However, when water becomes still, the sediment falls to the bottom, and everything is clearer. It is now possible to see what was previously invisible. A spiritual practice based on inward stillness and listening can work in a similar way. When lives are full of busyness, it is not easy to be aware of the Spirit within us. There is constant turmoil and movement, which muddies the waters of the inward landscape. How can people see things clearly when everything is cloudy and opaque? Stopping what they are doing, and becoming still and attentive, allows the sediment of their daily lives to sink down. This brings a greater sense of clarity. They can see things more clearly. What God is revealing to them becomes easier to recognize. Things they may have been avoiding are brought into view.

Pluralist Liberal Quaker Spirituality

Although the traditional Quaker approach to worship and spiritual practice emerged within an explicitly Christian context, it has proved amenable to a practice that looks beyond the Christian tradition and finds inspiration in a broader range of sources. In Pluralist Liberal Quakerism, which has developed in various places since the mid-twentieth century, the basic visible practices remain largely unchanged, but acceptable forms of belief and how Friends understand the source of their inward guidance have changed significantly. The Quaker emphasis on inward spiritual experience has enabled Friends to adopt a relatively receptive attitude to other faiths, and the assumption that true faith must be lived and not merely professed has produced doctrinal flexibility. Finally, and perhaps most significantly, their form of worship, based in silence, has provided a space within which a wide diversity of belief can coexist. This means that Pluralist Liberal Friends are united by what they do and how they do it, rather than by what they believe. This has been called the behavioral creed.[19]

Aspects of Pluralist Liberal Quakerism

Within worship and during personal spiritual practice, many Pluralist Liberal Friends focus on what they regard as a universal divine principle that is revealed in different ways in all the world's faiths.

Others feel led to interpret their spiritual experiences primarily with reference to one specific religious tradition or philosophy. Some combine Quaker practice with another religious affiliation. This form of multiple religious belonging has produced the phenomenon of "hyphenated Quakers" (e.g., Jewish-Quaker, Islamic-Quaker, and Anglican-Quaker).

Pluralism and Universalism

Modern Liberal Quakers have been strongly influenced by religious pluralism and universalism. Pluralism asserts that no one religious tradition has a monopoly on truth and that all faiths have value on their own terms. Universalism, in this case, implies that all religious traditions are diverse responses to a single source of spiritual inspiration developed within different times and places. There may be many paths, but each path, in its own way, leads to the same destination. The religious label is less important than the experience and how this is revealed in one's life. Hence, in communal worship and personal spiritual practice, many Friends feel that they are tapping into this universal source of inspiration. Others, while accepting pluralism and universalism, still find it helpful to concentrate on one tradition or approach. Here are some examples.

Buddhism

Many Pluralist Liberal Friends are attracted to Eastern meditation practices, especially those associated with Buddhism. Modern engaged Buddhism seems to be consistent with the Quaker conviction that one's inward experiences need to be outwardly embodied in one's life.[20] Buddhism offers contemplative practices and an ethical world view that is not dependent on either Christian belief or traditional theism. Some Friends identify as Buddhist Quakers or Quaker-Buddhists. Others simply use Buddhist meditation practices to center and still the mind in preparation for worship. Within Pluralist Liberal

Quaker worship and spiritual practice, this seems to enable people to remain open to a transcendent reality, without the need for a traditional conception of God. As Sallie King explains:

> Many Buddhist-friendly Quakers find the idea of Buddha Nature to have much in common with the Quaker idea of the Inner Light. Many, indeed, see these concepts as a place where Buddhism and Quakerism meet.[21]

Modern Paganism

Some Friends are inspired by modern forms of Paganism and value the way this diverse stream of contemporary spirituality offers an explicitly earth-centered and ecological world view. Modern Pagans tend to be pantheistic and polytheistic and often understand the divine in feminine terms. This can include a belief in animism, in which every part of creation is understood to be infused with spiritual energy. So, for example, in worship, a Quaker-Pagan like Cat Broome will seek to attend to this universal spiritual energy as the source of their guidance:

> I have come to believe, based on my experiences in worship, that the Spirit which I encounter in Quaker meeting is the same Spirit which my Christian Friends encounter and name "Christ." I don't call it that; I've never been prompted to by Spirit. But I do attempt to live my life faithfully in accordance to its leadings.[22]

Nontheism

During recent decades, some Friends have come to question traditional conceptions of God, and this has led to the development of a nontheist stream of Quaker spirituality. There is significant diversity within Quaker nontheism, but a common denominator is the rejection of any realist belief in a deity and especially in God as a creator and supreme ruler. Within this diversity, a few general tendencies can be seen. Some reject the use of God language altogether, while others are happy to use such language as metaphor, symbol, poetry, and so forth. Some adopt a robustly materialist worldview, while others are willing to remain open to mystery, uncertainty, and the unknown.[23] Sometimes, God is understood to symbolize the highest values and potential of humanity. However, the divine may also be viewed as "the entirety of what is known to exist in the physical universe."[24] This can lead to a focus in worship on interconnection and mystery, prompted by an awareness of the place of humanity within the enormity of the cosmos.

Pastoral and Evangelical Quaker Spirituality

If Liberal Friends retained an unprogrammed form of worship as they began to move away from an explicitly Christ-centered faith toward a more pluralist identity, Pastoral and Evangelical Friends began to adopt new worship practices in the 1870s, as they upheld biblical authority and orthodox Christian belief. While both Conservative and Liberal Friends value the quiet and contemplative aspects of early Quaker spirituality, Evangelical Friends have recovered its more emotionally expressive dimensions.[25] Those who were attracted to the Evangelical movement had two essential concerns about Quietist Quaker worship. Firstly, the practice did not seem to be sufficiently focused on the Bible and was vulnerable to a drift away from orthodox belief. Secondly, too often, the silence appeared to lack vitality and produced an atmosphere of spiritual deadness. For these Friends, the joyful singing and powerful preaching of the Methodists offered a more inspiring model. It is not surprising, therefore, that Evangelical Friends began to adopt a more programmed form of worship, including pre-planned sermons, hymns, and prayers. They still maintained an emphasis on a direct and inward relationship with God, resisted calls for the toleration of outward sacraments, and retained a space within services for spontaneous responses to the Holy Spirit.

Programmed and Semi-Programmed Worship

The form of worship adopted by Pastoral and Evangelical Friends looks like the practices of other Protestant churches, with a focus on reading the Scriptures, preaching, and simplified ritual. However, it also resembles the ways of other Spirit-led and charismatic churches. Silence may still have a place, but it is not dominant. This approach is described in the Richmond Declaration of Faith of 1887, which defined Evangelical Quaker belief and practice:

> Worship is the adoring response of the heart and mind to the influence of the Spirit of God. It stands neither in forms nor in the formal disuse of forms; it may be without words as well as with them, but it must be in spirit and in truth (John 4:24). We recognize the value of silence, not as an end but as a means toward the attainment of the end; a silence, not of listlessness or of vacant musing but of holy expectation before the Lord.[26]

So, while Friends practicing unprogrammed worship seek an experience of divine intimacy in silence alone, those who have adopted some programming in their worship supplement this with hymns, prayers, and other prepared words. For them, what matters is not so much the form as a transforming encounter with Christ through the Holy Spirit.[27] Any practice should help bring an awareness of the presence of Christ amid the gathered people. The predictability of programming is balanced by an openness to divine guidance and a willingness to change plans if prompted by the Holy Spirit. A Quaker pastor put it like this:

> For Friends, every meeting for worship is an adventure. Even when programming is planned, there needs to be a constant sensitivity to

the Spirit that frees us to joyfully discard or re-arrange the planned programming.[28]

Open Worship

Within liturgical forms of worship, the entire service culminates in the Eucharist. The hymns, prayers, and sermon prepare the worshippers for the sacramental sharing in the body and blood of Christ. In a similar way, the programmed aspects of Pastoral and Evangelical Quaker worship are understood to be a preparation for an inward encounter with God. This means that times of open worship within Quaker services are best understood as Holy Communion in the manner of Friends.

> By and large, Friends worship has a Protestant feel, but what distinguishes it is that the focus of the service is not the sermon, but the open worship—the period of silence that is sometimes very brief, but in some places takes up at least half the service.[29]

So, while Conservative and Liberal Friends feel that the best way to enter into communion with God is through unprogrammed worship as an extended practice of quiet waiting, Evangelical Friends believe that this experience is best achieved by a more active engagement with the Christian narrative through a programmed service that includes prayers, hymns, and a sermon. That said, currently, many programmed Friends are beginning to recover the use of unprogrammed worship within their services.

The Quaker Pastor

Although most Friends have identified and formally recorded ministers with a gift for communicating God's message, Pastoral and Evangelical Friends have taken this a step further in appointing paid pastors to serve their communities. It has been suggested that, compared to other churches, being a Quaker pastor is "the same, but different."[30] In particular, the need for constant openness to divine guidance makes the worship experience quite different for the Quaker pastor. They need to be able to discern the movement of the Holy Spirit within the worship and be open to the possibility that God's message for the community may be delivered through anyone present. In addition, the Quaker pastor accepts that their sermon may prompt Spirit-led responses from those present.

Evangelical Quaker Worship in the Majority World

Throughout much of their history, Friends were predominantly an English-speaking community concentrated in Britain and North America. However, during the past century, this has changed significantly, with substantial growth in other parts of the world, especially in East Africa and parts of South America. Most Friends now live within the Global South, and this is inevitably having an impact on Quaker worship styles, which are "increasingly textured by the practices, music, liturgies and theologies from cultures quite unlike those of its founders."[31] Such evolution involves a complex mix of factors. Initially, Western ways and assumptions were enforced in the newly established churches, but these have been adapted and amended over time under the influence of local traditions and cultures, and the wider Evangelical Christian context. In some cases, neglected patterns of Quaker worship have re-emerged in fresh ways. Whereas in North America, the influence of Evangelicalism tempered the traditional Quaker reticence about the use of music within worship, within emerging Quaker ways in the Global South, local cultures and traditions have undermined Western Evangelical antipathy toward dancing. This, along with the dominance of Pentecostalism within the wider religious culture, has produced a more embodied and charismatic form of Quaker worship, reflecting the ways of the earliest Friends. In addition, while the duration of

Quaker worship in the West has reduced over time, practices in the Global South are closer to the untimed and extended meetings for worship, common in the seventeenth century. Hence, there is both continuity and innovation in the worship practices of Friends within the majority world. One example of this is the "singing mysticism" of the Kenyan songwriter, Gideon W. H. Mweresa, whose music has made a significant contribution to the development of the Kenyan Quaker faith, drawing on traditional Luyia music and culture.[32] While Mweresa's music style reflected his local traditions, his words promoted orthodox Evangelical Quaker doctrine, with a strong emphasis on sin and the need for salvation.

Individual Spiritual Practices

Individual spiritual practices among Pastoral and Evangelical Friends utilize a range of disciplines shared with the wider Christian Church, including Bible study and prayer. Like other Friends, making space for times of retirement and paying attention to historic Quaker writings remain important, especially regarding pastoral epistles, spiritual journals, and autobiography. Such a holistic approach is reflected in the work of Evangelical Friend, Richard J. Foster, particularly in his book *Celebration of Discipline*, which is widely read by other Christians.[33] Foster promotes the classic disciplines of the Christian faith, dividing them into three themes: the inward disciplines of meditation, prayer, fasting, and study; the outward disciplines of simplicity, solitude, submission, and service; and the corporate disciplines of confession, worship, guidance, and celebration.

So, whether Friends are Evangelical Christians or Pluralist Liberals, and whether their worship is silent and unprogrammed or emotionally expressive and programmed, the essential purpose of Quaker worship and spiritual practice is to nurture a deepening sense of God's presence and an experience of divine guidance, so that what is revealed inwardly and spiritually can be embodied outwardly in a new way of life and a transformed world.

Notes

1. Donald K. McKim, *Westminster Dictionary of Theological Terms* (Louisville, KY: Westminster John Knox Press, 1996), 307.
2. Maurice Creasey, "Worship in the Christian Tradition," in *Collected Essays of Maurice Creasey, 1912–2004*, ed. David L. Johns (Lampeter: Edwin Mellen Press, 2011), 167–87.
3. Edward Burrough, "Epistle to the Reader," in *The Great Mystery of the Great Whore Unfolded*, ed. George Fox (1659). Quoted in Britain Yearly Meeting, *Quaker Faith and Practice*, 19.20.
4. Francis Howgill, "Testimony Concerning Edward Burrough," in *The Memorable Works of a Son of Thunder*, ed. Edward Burrough (1672). Quoted in Britain Yearly Meeting, *Quaker Faith and Practice*, 19.08.
5. Ohio Yearly Meeting (Conservative), *The Book of Discipline* (Barnesville, OH: Ohio Yearly Meeting Conservative, 2001), 7.
6. Arthur Berk et al., *Traditional Quaker Christianity* (Barnesville, OH: Ohio Yearly Meeting Conservative, 2014), 81.
7. North Carolina Yearly Meeting (Conservative), *Faith and Practice* (Greensboro, NC: North Carolina Yearly Meeting Conservative, 1983), 13.
8. Beatrix Saxon Snell, *A Joint and Visible Fellowship* (Wallingford, PA: Pendle Hill Pamphlet 140, 1965), 10.
9. Brent J. Bill, *Holy Silence: The Gift of Quaker Spirituality* (Brewster, MA: Paraclete Press, 2005), 91.
10. Margery Post Abbott, *To Be Broken and Tender: A Quaker Theology for Today* (Whittier, CA: Friend Bulletin Corporation, 2010).
11. Patricia Loring, *Listening Spirituality: Volume I, Personal Spiritual Practices Among Friends* (Washington Grove, MD: Openings Press, 1997).

12 Michael Birkel, *Silence and Witness: The Quaker Tradition* (London: Darton, Longman and Todd, 2004), 78.
13 Bill, *Holy Silence*, 37–8.
14 Thomas Kelly, *A Testament of Devotion* (London: Quaker Home Service, 1979), 60–1.
15 North Carolina Yearly Meeting (Conservative), *Faith and Practice*, 28.
16 John Woolman, and Phillips P. Moulton, eds., *The Journal and Major Essays of John Woolman* (Richmond, IN: Friends United Press, 1989), 53–4.
17 Barclay, *Apology*, 76.
18 George Fox's epistles are available to view online here: https://qbi.earlham.edu/gfe/index.htm (17 September 2024).
19 Pink Dandelion, The Liturgies of Quakerism (Aldershot: Ashgate, 2004), 93.
20 See, for example, Valerie Brown, *The Mindful Quaker: A Brief Introduction to Buddhist Wisdom for Friends* (Wallingford, PA: Pendle Hill Publications, 2006).
21 Sallie B. King, "Liberal Quakers and Buddhism," in *Quakers and Mysticism: Comparative and Syncretic Approaches to Spirituality*, ed. John R. Kershner (Basingstoke: Palgrave Macmillan, 2019), 231.
22 Cat Broome, "About," Quaker Pagan Reflections blog, https://www.patheos.com/blogs/quakerpagan/about (accessed October 20, 2023).
23 David Boulton, ed., *Godless for God's Sake: Nontheism in Contemporary Quakerism* (Cumbria: DHM Quaker Books, 2006), 8.
24 Randazzo, "Quakers and Non-Theism," 286.
25 Anderson, *Following Jesus*, 56.
26 The Richmond Declaration of Faith (1887) quoted in *Faith & Practice of Indiana Yearly Meeting of the Religious Society of Friends* (Richmond, IN: Indiana Yearly Meeting, 2018), 30.
27 Anderson, *Following Jesus*, 58.
28 Phil Baisley, *The Same But Different: Ministry and the Quaker Pastor* (Richmond, IN: Friends Unite Press, 2018), 34.
29 John Punshon, *Reasons for Hope: The Faith and Future of the Friends Church* (Richmond, IN: Friends United Press, 2001), 80.

30 Baisley, *The Same, But Different*, 31.
31 David L. Johns, "Worship and Sacraments," in *The Oxford Handbook of Quaker Studies*, ed. Stephen W. Angell and Pink Dandelion (Oxford: Oxford University Press, 2013), 273.
32 Esther Mombo, "The Singing Mysticism: Kenyan Quakerism, the Case of Gideon W. H. Mweresa," in *Quakers and Mysticism: Comparative and Syncretic Approaches to Spirituality*, ed. Jon R. Kershner (Basingstoke: Palgrave Macmillan, 2019), 201–19.
33 Richard J. Foster, *Celebration of Discipline: The Path to Spiritual Growth* (London: Hodder and Stoughton, 2008).

4

The Testing

Quaker Discernment and Decision-Making

Introduction

In all the diverse expressions of Quaker spirituality, significant emphasis is given to an intimate inward relationship with God, continuing revelation, and the experience of divine guidance. Quakers believe that God is still speaking today and that true worship is based on a practice of listening, hearing, and obeying that voice. Given that Friends seek to follow the inward leadings of the Holy Spirit, how does this impact on how they make decisions, both as individuals and as a community? This chapter explores Quaker decision-making as a discipline of spiritual discernment. How do Friends distinguish between the voice of God and other impulses and motivations? What is distinctive about the Quaker approach to decision-making?

Discernment and Quaker Spirituality

The discipline of discernment is a practice of sorting and analyzing things to distinguish between what is true and what is false. In spiritual terms, it is used to determine God's will by judging whether an idea or motivation is divinely inspired or not. Discernment, therefore, requires Friends to respond to their religious experiences by interrogating their emotions and motivations. Any individual or group that claims to act on divine guidance must take this practice seriously. Throughout history, those committing evil actions have often claimed that they were doing God's will. An essential feature of the Quaker way is the conviction that inward divine guidance is available to everyone and that this guidance should govern people's lives. Therefore, discernment is an essential safeguard protecting individuals and communities from the dangers of delusion or self-centered motivations. It is more of an art than a science, and Friends have found that as people develop and grow spiritually, their powers of discernment grow too.[1]

Discernment within Christianity

The earliest Christian Church was a prophetic movement. The gift of the Holy Spirit meant that all believers could become the agents of God. People expected to receive revelations because they believed that God was still speaking. In such circumstances, how a divine message might be distinguished from a human motivation became a significant issue. The apostle Paul wrote to the church in Rome, "Do not be conformed to this age, but be transformed by the renewing of the mind, so that you may discern what is the will of God" (Rom. 12:2). The ways of the world and the will of God are often incompatible, and the believer needs to be able to differentiate between the two. The author of the first letter of John advised his readers, "do not believe every spirit, but test the spirits to see whether they are from God, for many false prophets have gone out into the world" (1 Jn 4:1). Discernment was necessary, not only to test one's own experiences, but also to prevent the community from being led astray by bogus teachers. Discernment became important within the Western monastic tradition through the works of writers such as John Cassian and Benedict of Nursia.[2] Cassian recognized the human capacity for self-delusion and self-interest. In such circumstances, the practice of discernment, based on a healthy suspicion about personal motivations, was essential if people were to be aligned with the divine will.[3] In the sixteenth century, the founder of the Jesuits, Ignatius of Loyola, offered rules for discernment in his "Spiritual Exercises," including the close examination of inner motivations to determine the will of God in making decisions.[4] He encouraged an awareness of one's disposition, whether it was life-giving or destructive, and counseled people to give attention to the potential implications of their actions.[5] Finally, although Protestants have not tended to give significant attention to discernment, some modern Pentecostal and charismatic Christians have recognized its importance, because prophecy can be a mixture of human and divine and needs to be tested to assess its authenticity.[6]

Discernment and Traditional Quaker Spirituality

The earliest Friends were inspired by the New Testament vision of the Church as a temple of living stones and the Body of Christ. The community becomes a temple of living stones when Christ, the eternal high priest, dwells within it. He is the one in whom God and humanity, creator and creation, and heaven and earth meet. This makes divine guidance possible. If the Church is to be healthy and function well, the body must be controlled by its head. How can the gathered body ensure that it is being ruled by Christ? This vision forms the basis of the Quaker understanding of discernment and decision-making. The living body and the living temple must become a community in which Christ dwells and through which Christ acts. Since all decisions must be handed over to God, the gathered people need to be faithful in discerning the divine will. This is described as follows:

> Since Jesus Christ is head of the church and present among us as our Teacher and Guide, we commit ourselves to listening to and obeying Him. In our manner of worship and decision making and

in the way we order ourselves as a church, we continue to learn how to better listen to and obey Christ together.[7]

The traditional Quaker approach to discernment and decision-making also assumes that the whole creation is divinely ordered. This is a "gospel order." Although humanity lost sight of this order and became a disruptive presence within creation, due to the work of Christ, it has again become possible for people to be aligned with it. Quaker practice is an attempt to bring the life of the community into alignment with gospel order, based on the conviction that this order "can be discerned by human beings who seek it out."[8]

The Nature and Practice of Quaker Discernment

Friends recognize the value of developing a keen awareness of the dangers of self-deception, stressing the need for internal vigilance. Everyone is expected to contribute to a shared practice of listening, hearing, and obeying, rather than merely focusing on their own individual preferences. Discernment demands humility and patience. Everyone must surrender their own will and commit themselves to being attentive to the movement of the Spirit. This requires real mutual trust within the community and a conviction that everyone is acting with integrity. To be sensitive to the Spirit, Friends must be willing to set aside their normal thoughts and preoccupations. Such a discipline involves looking backward to scrutinize where emotions and responses are arising from and looking forward to determine what God is calling us to do. This means becoming increasingly alert to what usually motivates them as individuals and groups.

Becoming Aware of Emotions and Responses

In the discernment process, the aim is to allow God to direct one's decision-making, rather than it being driven by self-centered or socially conditioned human responses and emotions. Developing a heightened sensitivity to feelings and reactions as they arise means that these motivations are less likely to control people, and they are better able to set them aside in seeking God's will. Friends might ask themselves: What gut reactions and assumptions are driving me? Can I become aware of them and where they emerge from? To what extent are they rooted in unconscious assumptions? Asking these sorts of questions can help people improve their self-awareness so that such responses don't dominate them.

There are many different dimensions to this. A person's upbringing, social context, and personality type often shape their responses to things. As humans grow up, they absorb the norms and values of their family, their friends, and the wider culture. This socialization tends to establish certain assumptions about what is viewed as normal or abnormal and what is acceptable or unacceptable. For example, White people of European origin have been socialized into assumptions rooted in a long history of colonialism and racism. These can instinctively shape the way a person responds to different cultures and ethnic groups. In addition, different personality types can shape responses in a variety of ways. Gaining some awareness of personal preferences and orientations can help people further scrutinize their reactions. When Friends are unaware of these factors, they may be quietly informing their decisions in unconscious ways. This will hamper their ability to hear the still, small voice of God and limit the quality of their discernment. If such attitudes remain hidden and unquestioned blind spots, then aspects of the dominant culture are likely to drive the decisions they make. These prejudices can be extremely damaging, especially when they are reinforced by dominant social power structures.

When interrogating their motivations, questions Friends might ask could include: how do I respond to new ideas and situations that seem strange to me? Am I aware of my gut reactions and what prompts them? How do I respond to people who are not like me? If I strongly identify with one group, are my responses to others fair and balanced or are they shaped by socialization? How far am I able to sit lightly on strongly held opinions? Can I find a way to set them aside while trying to make decisions? It is common for people to experience feelings of love and hate or joy and anger. Friends might reflect on what generates these emotional reactions. Awareness and honesty can moderate their influence and help everyone contribute more positively to discernment and decision-making. This is not about losing a sense of personal identity or giving up on cherished values and beliefs. It is about people becoming increasingly conscious of the things that drive them, so they are more open to divine guidance as the essential basis of personal and communal decision-making.

The External Tests

In addition to exercising caution about the possible influence of self-centered assumptions and inclinations on the discernment process, Friends have also recognized the contribution that certain external tests can make in ensuring that decision-making is genuinely divinely led. Although these tests have varied over time and in different situations, it is possible to identify a few enduring methods. The first and primary test has been the practice of discernment itself, the interpretation of divine revelation as it is experienced in worship and personal practice. This can be done by individuals, but it has greater weight when undertaken within the community. The Quaker focus on experience makes the interrogation of human emotions and responses essential within Quaker spirituality.

Throughout history, most Friends have regarded the Bible, when illuminated by the Spirit, as the most significant external test in discerning divine guidance, in which Christ is the essential role model and standard of faith. Friends have believed that the Holy Spirit enables them to embody the way of Jesus and that there will be consistency between the Jesus of the Scriptures and the Jesus revealed in the lives of his people. The essential biblical accounts of the teachings of Jesus, such as the Sermon on the Mount (Mt. 5–7), have offered Friends a valuable benchmark when assessing their own leadings. The apostle Paul's description of the fruits of the Spirit (Gal. 5:22-23) has provided another significant measure of authenticity. Is the shared sense of guidance leading the people to love, joy, peace, patience, kindness, generosity, faithfulness, gentleness, and self-control? Friends have also asserted that the guidance of the Holy Spirit will be constant and dependable over time. Hence, the decisions and commitments of past generations usually act as a helpful test for discernment in the present. The enduring shape of Quaker testimony can also provide a reliable measure for assessing the legitimacy of current leadings. Friends' long-standing witness to peace, truthfulness, integrity, and justice, reflecting Paul's fruits of the Spirit, offers another measure within the discernment process. True leadings will endure, even when obstacles are put in their way, so patience and the test of time also function as essential tests. Finally, within Quaker spirituality, the ultimate test of a true leading is the ability of the community to come into unity. When this occurs after giving a matter prayerful and patient consideration, there is a general sense that the guidance of the Holy Spirit has become clear.

In their religious context, the earliest Friends were reacting against what they perceived to be an overemphasis on the authority of tradition and Scripture and instead stressed the importance of a living faith based on the direct guidance of the Holy Spirit. Over time, this general attitude has been maintained, but in practice, Quaker discernment has taken account of both the Bible and tradition. Over time, different expressions of the Quaker way have prioritized different foundations for discernment: Conservative Friends have emphasized the quietist disciplines of human surrender and watchfulness; Evangelical Friends have asserted the centrality of Scripture; and Liberal Friends have stressed the preeminence of reason and individual experience.[9] While Quakers have asserted that the leadings of the Holy Spirit will be consistent, in practice, interpretation of this guidance has varied in different places and times. An openness to fresh insights is particularly marked among Liberal Friends, who tend to believe that God's guidance is revealed more and more clearly over time.

Communal Discernment and Decision-Making

The way Friends order their communal decision-making is a unique and distinctive feature of the Quaker way, reflecting a commitment to the rule of God in human affairs. The basic structures and practices that were developed in the seventeenth century have stood the test of time and continue to be used today. A key challenge was to ensure good order without re-establishing human authority structures that might undermine divine leadership. Quaker organization is based on a hierarchy of meetings, in which each level reflects how often it meets to conduct communal business. This has produced monthly meetings locally and yearly meetings at the geographical level. The way authority works within these structures varies. In some cases, it is the yearly meeting that holds the ultimate authority. In others, there is a more complex distribution of authority between monthly and yearly meetings, and those meetings established in between them. Overall, however, Quaker organizational structures tend to resemble an inverted pyramid. This means that as a matter under consideration rises through the structure of meetings, the more Friends are involved in the process, implying a greater level of authority. In the past, involvement in yearly meetings was more restricted, but today, participation is usually open to all members.

The Meeting for Worship for Church Affairs

Friends seek to make decisions as a community within the context of worship. In a meeting for worship for church affairs, this means adopting an attitude of stillness and attentiveness to discern God's will for a particular matter under consideration. The community aims to achieve a common understanding of where God is leading them. Such a practice is therefore subtly different from consensus-based decision-making. Because the focus is on divine guidance, the discipline requires everyone to surrender their own ideas and opinions. Friends are disinclined to give too much weight to individual contributions employing clever argument or persuasive eloquence. A meeting for worship for church affairs is not a debate. There should be no lobbying, and decisions are not made by a majority vote. The central concern is to ensure that a spirit of worship is maintained, which allows God to lead the process. This demands a serious commitment to prayerful listening and a willingness to exercise patience.[10]

> our task is not to find a decision of which we all approve, but the decision which is in unity with the Holy Spirit. We have arrived at the correct decision not when there is consensus or effective unanimity, but when the Spirit within us witnesses that the decision is correct.[11]

While those present may offer spoken contributions, as vocal ministry, everyone must test their desire to speak. Does this urge come from themselves or from God? Is this the right time to speak? It is important that the sense of being in worship is not lost by slipping into discussion or argument. The discernment of divine guidance cannot be rushed. Any pressure to get the business done quickly is treated with caution, as this may reflect a lack of commitment to the discipline. To be genuinely attentive to divine guidance, participants in these meetings need to come with open minds and sit lightly on their preconceived views. It is hard to discern God's will when already invested in a preferred outcome. This does not mean that factual information and the advice of experts play no part. Spirit-led decision-making always addresses specific circumstances and issues. Gathering necessary information, listening to a wide range of contributions, and carefully weighing their relevance are essential aspects of the process.

Within a meeting for church affairs, clerks coordinate the conduct of the business. They take a particular responsibility for discernment, trying to sense how the Spirit is moving among the gathered people, and call individuals indicating a desire to speak. The clerk's role is supported by the sense of God's presence, the assistance of the elders, and the spiritual upholding of the other members of the meeting. A decision is made when those present feel they are in unity about a matter under consideration, and this has been reflected accurately in a written minute drafted by the clerk. The minute describes the community's understanding of God's will at that time. This is called the "sense of the meeting." Not everyone will necessarily agree, and it is important to ensure that the views of those who dissent have been heard and considered. It is always possible that the minority position reflects the will of God. Those who do not agree with a decision are faced with two choices: they can stand firm in their opposition to the proposed minute, in which case the matter may be deferred, or they can stand aside, allowing the minute to be approved. The clerk and recording clerk must exercise spiritual judgement and continually assess the sense of the meeting and whether the time is right to share a draft minute with those present. When a draft minute is read, if unity is not achieved, further discernment will be required. If the community feels close to unity, suggestions for minor amendments to the minute may be made before it is submitted again. When clerks ask the meeting if a minute is acceptable, Friends indicate their approval in a variety of ways. This method of decision-making is by no means infallible. God is omniscient, but people are not. If subsequently a decision is found to have been made in error, this does not necessarily invalidate the process. It might reflect human limitations and an inadequate application of the discipline. Yearly meetings draft and circulate epistles describing the experience.

The Quaker approach to decision-making seems to have drawn on New Testament models, especially the process adopted during the Council of Jerusalem (Acts 15:6-28). The meeting was called to determine whether Gentile converts should have to follow all the requirements of Mosaic Law, especially circumcision. Time was made available for those present to express their views. The gathered apostles and elders remained silent and listened to Barnabas and Paul (v. 12). James took the role of clerk, and the words he spoke sound like the reading of a draft minute for consideration (v. 13-21). There was a clear sense that the decision was discerned under the guidance of the Holy Spirit, tested against the Scriptures, and achieved not by voting but by coming into unity. God had given them the answer, and the resulting epistle seems to confirm this (v. 28).

Threshing Meetings

When Friends are grappling with a complex, challenging, or controversial issue, they sometimes use a threshing meeting as part of the discernment and decision-making process. The imagery of threshing is drawn from the agricultural practice of beating gathered cereal crops to separate the edible grain from the straw. In the Bible, it is sometimes used as a metaphor for distinguishing between good and evil (e.g., Mt. 3:12). Within modern Quakerism, the word threshing is most often applied to a practice that enables Friends to explore an issue thoroughly to identify and separate out what is relevant or useful from what is unimportant or unhelpful. In a threshing meeting, everyone is encouraged to express their feelings and views freely and fully, so that nothing important remains hidden or unspoken. It is an ordered but free-flowing activity which allows an issue to be explored as thoroughly as possible, as preparation for the quieter and more prayerful approach adopted within a normal meeting for worship for church affairs. Friends have found that the threshing process helps the members of the community to discern their response to a particular matter more effectively, as they seek to come into unity together.

The Discernment of Gifts and Ministries

The identification of spiritual gifts is an important part of Quaker discernment. The community has a critical role in identifying, naming, and nurturing the spiritual gifts of all its members and then encouraging them to use these gifts in the service of Friends and the world. This focus on gifts is closely linked to the Quaker understanding of ministry. Ministry is essentially a form of service that requires God-given gifts. Since all Friends have gifts, everyone has a potential ministry. For early Friends, this position reflected the apostle Paul's description of the church as a community of diverse gifts (1 Corinthians 12). To be healthy and function effectively, a body needs many different organs that work seamlessly together. The faith community needs this too. Individuals are not always aware of their own gifts, and so others need to be able to discern them and point them out. This is best done where Friends know each other deeply and share bonds of love and trust. It is God who grants each individual their gifts, and through worshipful attention, it is God who will reveal them in others. Everyone has a part to play in this, but some Friends, such as elders and nominations committee members, take particular responsibility for discernment in this area. Based on their gifts, nominations committees seek to match people to various roles and responsibilities. Across history, Friends have appointed elders who look after the spiritual life of the community and recorded ministers who have a gift for conveying divine messages. In addition, some individuals have been recognized as "weighty Friends," whose guidance and opinion are particularly valued because of their spiritual maturity and sensitivity to the movement of the Spirit.

Discernment as a Personal Practice

Within Quaker spirituality, the commitment to seeking God's will through a practice of quiet attentiveness and discernment is not confined to communal activities alone. It is also a discipline that individuals should apply in all aspects of their lives. Those who are serious about this practice will seek to discern divine guidance moment by moment, hour by hour, and day by day. This is particularly important for an individual when approaching major life decisions such as the kind of work they will do, whether they should marry and/or have children, or get involved in social action. Tried and tested Quaker practices can be extremely valuable in these situations. Within a Quaker context, individual Friends are not expected to make these decisions alone. The community is there to offer love, support, gentle challenge, and testing. This reflects a sense of interdependence that is sometimes neglected within a culture dominated by individualism. Let us look at some examples.

Discerning the Call to Vocal Ministry

In Quaker worship, anyone may speak if they feel prompted to do so. While some people find themselves on their feet without any conscious decision and may not remember what they say, others "sit with" their message to be sure it is from God. Testing the urge to speak is a good example of individual spiritual discernment. When a Friend feels this urge, they are encouraged to apply several tests before rising to speak. One set of questions interrogates the source and purpose of the message. Is it coming from me or from God? Is it arising from a deep place, or does it reflect my usual thoughts? Is it only for my benefit, or for the benefit of the whole community? Is this the right time and the right place to share the message? A second set of questions is more about assessing the motivation to speak. Do I feel a strong and growing sense of compulsion? If I resist the urge to speak, does it persist or begin to fade? Am I reluctant to speak due to a lack of confidence or a sense of unworthiness? Am I being faithful in what God is calling me to do? In common with all forms of discernment, there is no guarantee of getting it right. However, good discernment can help guard against the dangers of speaking too frequently and superficially or failing to respond to a genuine divine leading.

Testing Individual Concerns in Community

There are important interconnections between individual discernment and the discernment of the community. For example, a Friend may seek to test a particular leading or concern with others. This is usually done for three main reasons: (1) they want Friends to support them in doing something; (2) they want the community to recognize their concern and act on it corporately; or (3) they simply wish to involve Friends in their decision-making, as a matter of mutual accountability. This kind of discernment can be done in small groups, but it might also be done through the established structure of meetings from the local to the top level. In some instances, this forms part of established processes, such as applications for membership or marriages. In all cases, at the small group level, Friends can make use of clearness committees.

Clearness Committees

Initially, clearness committees were established to enable Friends to work with couples in testing an intention to marry under the care of a Quaker meeting. In recent times, they have been used more generally to help individuals explore a personal dilemma or do preliminary testing before taking a matter to a meeting for church affairs. This is a small group practice that aims to uphold and support a Friend seeking clearness about an issue. The purpose is not for the committee to try and come up with a solution. Instead, they seek to enable the individual to think more deeply about the matter under divine guidance. The number of meetings required and the length of each session will vary, but enough time needs to be set aside to allow everyone to consider the question in a deep and prayerful way. The whole process should be conducted in the spirit of worship, avoiding slipping into conversation and including periods of waiting in silence and stillness. Sufficient information about the situation needs to be shared so that everyone has a clear appreciation of the issue being discerned. A significant portion of the meeting should be reserved for quiet reflection and listening for divine guidance. Much like vocal ministry, committee members may share any reflections or open questions that arise within them. If possible, these should be recorded so that the person can take them away for further consideration. Over the years, Friends have found this to be a powerful and effective way to aid individual discernment and decision-making.

So, while Friends have always emphasized the experience of spiritual intimacy and the possibility of receiving divine guidance, they have sought to test and regulate this using the discipline of discernment. Discernment, therefore, acts as an essential link between inward spiritual experience and how it is reflected in the lives of Friends, individually and collectively. In Quaker spirituality, the true fruit of an inner life centered on God is a Christ-like life within the world. Friends have called this outward manifestation of their inward experiences their witness or testimony. The next chapter looks at this aspect of the Quaker way in more detail.

Notes

1. John Punshon, *Testimony and Tradition: Some Aspects of Quaker Spirituality* (London: Quaker Home Service, 1990), 14.
2. Michael Birkel, "Leadings and Discernment," in *The Oxford Handbook of Quaker Studies*, ed. Stephen W. Angell and Pink Dandelion (Oxford: Oxford University Press, 2013), 246.
3. Peter Tyler, "Christian Spiritual Direction," in *The Bloomsbury Guide to Christian Spirituality*, ed. Richard Woods and Peter Tyler (London: Bloomsbury, 2012), 202.
4. Birkel, "Leadings and Discernment," 246.
5. Tyler, "Christian Spiritual Direction," 204.
6. Mark J. Cartledge, "Charismatic Spirituality" in Woods and Tyler, *The Bloomsbury Guide to Christian Spirituality*, 219.
7. Northwest Yearly Meeting, *Faith and Practice* (Newberg, OR: Northwest Yearly Meeting, 2021), 18.
8. Lloyd Lee Wilson, *Essays on the Quaker Vision of Gospel Order* (Burnsville, NC: Celo Valley Books, 1993), 132.
9. Birkel, "Leadings and Discernment," 252–3.
10. Michael J. Sheeran, *Beyond Majority Rule: Voteless Decisions in the Religious Society of Friends* (Philadelphia, PA: Philadelphia Yearly Meeting, 1996).
11. Wilson, *Gospel Order*, 133.

5

The Outward Quaker Testimony

Introduction

> True godliness does not turn men out of the world but enables them to live better in it and excites their endeavours to mend it.[1]

Although Friends have placed great emphasis on the inward and spiritual dimensions of their faith, this does not mean that Quaker spirituality is essentially inward-looking and detached from reality. Indeed, inward experience is inextricably linked to individual and communal conduct. Friends seek to integrate spiritual practice with social action. The term "testimony" draws on a courtroom analogy. A witness is someone who gives a testimony to a court about what they have seen or heard. For Friends, this testimony is about embodying inward divine guidance in their outward lives. Quaker testimony has five essential characteristics: it is a response to a divine leading, rather than a human value or principle; it only exists to the extent to which it is visibly enacted; it reflects the life of the whole community, rather than just individual actions; it tends to be discomforting because it challenges accepted norms and assumptions; and since its source is divine love, it is concerned for the well-being of other humans, animals, and the rest of creation.[2] Quaker testimony is rooted in the things that are eternal, but is always enacted in specific situations. It must be worked out on a case-by-case basis and therefore cannot be fully predicted in advance.

The General Character of Quaker Testimony

A more detailed examination of the general nature of Quaker testimony may be helpful before considering how Friends have lived their faith in diverse ways across history.

Divine Command and Faithful Response

The Quaker discipline of being still and listening to God prompts a sense of divine guidance, which, when discerned carefully, needs to be put into practice. Divine command should lead to a faithful response. Since the source of testimony is an encounter with God, it has a prophetic quality. Visible action is an embodied form of communication. This reflects the Quaker conviction that the inward and the outward are fundamentally interconnected. Inward spiritual condition is reflected in outward lives, and each person's actions influence their spiritual state. However, testimony is not an indicator of worthiness, it is the divine nature revealed in human conduct. It is an experience of God breaking into the particularities of human lives, disquieting their hearts so that they will not become still until a response is forthcoming.[3]

Embodying the way of Jesus

> *You are my friends if you do what I command you.* (Jn 15:14)

Early Friends believed they were experiencing Christ returning in Spirit within them as their teacher, priest, and king. It is not surprising, therefore, that Quaker testimony has tended to have a distinctly Christ-centered flavor. When people live "in the same kind of relationship with the risen Christ that had transformed the lives of the apostles and the early church,"[4] they will visibly embody the way of Jesus. This has not just meant following his teachings as they are recorded in the Bible. It has also reflected the experience of Christ ruling within his people and living through them. Friends have felt that what the historical Jesus taught in the first century, the living Spirit of Christ would reveal within them today.

A Glimpse of Heaven on Earth

Their life-changing spiritual experiences convinced the earliest Friends that God was acting to establish the kingdom of heaven and that they were being involved in this process. They seem to have been given a glimpse of heaven on earth and were determined to share this with the rest of the world.[5] As a result, Quaker testimony has had a strongly eschatological flavor, pointing to the fulfillment of God's promises and how things will be in the end. Although these early expectations were not realized, Friends have continued to believe that divine rule can be made visible in the lives of the faithful. God's kingdom has come in part but will eventually come in fullness. The agents of the kingdom are those who are attentive to divine guidance and faithful in carrying it out. They are witnesses offering a testimony to God's love, justice, and mercy in every aspect of life. It is not just about heroic forms of public action, it can also include the small-scale, personal dimensions of life. For example, the family can become an essential practice ground for the heavenly life.[6]

Negative and Positive Testimony

Quaker testimony displays both negative and positive characteristics.[7] At first, it tends to be a negative response to specific human behaviors and social arrangements that seem to conflict with divine guidance. This prompts actions that interrupt and refuse to go along with such behaviors and social arrangements, even when Friends are not always clear about what an alternative way might look like. It has been suggested that this represents a practice of "doing the truth." It is "a sustained enacted opposition to some power or structure of thought that claims to shape and uphold the world but in fact destroys it."[8] Usually, the negative dimension of testimony leads to a more positive response. Having rejected something, Friends seek to offer an alternative to it. This involves trying out new ways of living or organizing society. So, a testimony against something leads to innovation, offering a vision of positive change more aligned with the divine will. Such holy experiments are about living adventurously, not quite knowing what the outcome will be.[9] Two illustrative examples are examined below: the human use of violence and the relationship with the rest of creation.

Humans and Violence

The assumption that violence must be used to safeguard peace and justice is deeply embedded in human culture. This has been called the "myth of redemptive violence."[10] Because this view is often taken for granted, it seems uncontroversial; it is simply common sense. However, the use of violence always perpetuates violence and may ultimately fail to secure enduring peace and justice. Friends have found that divine guidance leads them to interrupt and refuse to go along with ways of organizing things based on violence and coercion. For them, a deeper divine truth counters accepted human wisdom. In a negative testimony, Friends have often been conscientious objectors during times of war, campaigning against militarism and the arms trade and resisting human structures that use physical force. In positive testimony, they have tried to live peaceably in their own lives, supporting diplomacy aimed at avoiding war, actively engaging in conflict transformation and peace-building initiatives, and promoting nonviolent methods of political action.

Humans and Creation

The idea that humans are superior to the rest of creation and have a right to rule over it has been a widely held conviction, especially within Western societies. Linked to this is the belief that the natural world is simply a source of material resources for humans to exploit for their own purposes, that other animals exist primarily for human benefit, and that amassing wealth and personal possessions is the key indicator of success. A growing awareness of the deepening ecological crisis threatening human existence has meant that these assumptions are increasingly called into question. The negative testimony of Friends involves a rejection of this worldview, including a refusal to participate, as far as possible, in destructive and unsustainable behavior, and political action calling for essential changes to the economic system. This is based on a recognition that all things are interconnected, that human well-being depends on the rest of the natural world, and that other animals are God's creatures, worthy of respect, care, and compassion. In positive terms, Friends seek to live simpler lives based on sufficiency rather than excessive wealth, change their diets and modes of transport, and contribute to the development of more sustainable models of social, political, and economic organization. Of course, none of this is peculiar to Friends, but their approaches have a distinctly Quaker flavor.

Testimony as Provocative and Risky Communication

One way Friends have sought to promote awareness of the Quaker way is through the visible example of their lives. Such embodied testimony is regarded as an essential method of communicating the faith. In 1656, writing from Launceston jail, in Cornwall, George Fox counseled Friends to:

> Be patterns, be examples in all countries, places, islands, nations, wherever you come, that your carriage and life may preach among

all sorts of people, and to them; then you will come to walk cheerfully over the world, answering that of God in everyone.[11]

Fox was convinced that when human behavior is motivated by divine guidance and properly discerned, it can reach out to others, prompting an awareness of the presence of the Holy Spirit, which can transform them, if they are willing to pay attention and follow its leadings. This means that Quaker testimony presents itself to the world as a form of nonviolent communication. Although it is provocative and seeks a response from others, testimony rejects coercion, and observers are free to interpret it as they see fit. This makes it a risky enterprise. Testimony can easily be misunderstood and misrepresented. It may have unintended consequences, leading to humiliation and suffering. In addition, in retrospect, Friends may feel that what they have done was unhelpful or wrong in some way.[12]

Discernment, Mutual Support, and Accountability

Because testimony is such a crucial aspect of Quaker identity and may well involve public witness that is risky and costly, serious attention must be given to discernment, mutual support, and accountability. The test of discernment is required to find clearness about what needs to be done, how it should be done, and who should do it. As noted above, because Friends give significant emphasis to divine guidance, discernment acts as an essential safeguard. Indeed, when prophetic words and actions have been carefully discerned by the community, they gain power and authority and are more likely to have the desired impact. While the shape of past testimony acts as a useful guide, this is not sufficient because current circumstances may be different. Accountability applies to both individuals and the whole group. Individual Friends have a responsibility to take account of communal decisions in the way they live their lives and to bring their concerns and leadings to the community for testing and discernment. The community will then feel able to provide those "acting under concern" with spiritual support and practical assistance. In this way, effective discernment, mutual support, and accountability help Friends to live faithfully within the world, knowing they are following in the footsteps of their forebears, and walking the way of a spirit-led people who express their inward experiences in their outward lives.

The Overall Shape of Quaker Testimony

During the twentieth century, some Friends began to use short lists of core testimonies. This can be helpful in summarizing the enduring shape of Quaker values across time. However, it risks turning testimony, as a particular response to divine guidance within specific circumstances, into what looks more like a rigid set of universal values that are separate from one another and thus optional. It is also clear that the interpretation of these testimonies has developed and changed over time and in different places. One commonly used list employs the acronym S.P.I.C.E.S.:

Simplicity

The simplicity testimony is a commitment to organizing lives in a way that avoids distractions, helping Friends to focus on what is most important, the discipline of listening for and responding to divine guidance. What is it in their lives that gets in the way of this essential practice? Unhelpful distractions might include excessive busyness, the desire to accumulate material wealth, and an undue concern for personal image and reputation.

Peace

The peace testimony is a conviction that God's way, as it is revealed in Christ, is a way of peace that rejects the use of coercive force and violent conflict. For nearly four hundred years, Quakers have sought to resist war and practice nonviolence, peacebuilding, and conflict transformation. Along with various Anabaptist groups, Friends are one of the Historic Peace Churches.

Integrity

The integrity testimony emphasizes the need for continuity between what is said and done. Are Friends trustworthy and truthful, or dishonest and hypocritical? Do they try to maintain conduct that is consistent in all areas of their lives, or do they adopt a variety of roles in different circumstances in a way that is insincere and deceptive?

Community

This testimony recognizes that the community is more than just a group of individuals. While affirming the value of each person, Friends know that doing things together as a people is important. In a community, they are more than the sum of their parts and can have a greater impact on the world. This means acknowledging interdependence and building bonds of mutual support and accountability.

Equality

The equality testimony is an affirmation of the dignity and worth of all people. This commitment pays attention to what people share in common, as well as their diversity and differences. In the context of inequality and injustice, it is inspired by the way Jesus showed particular concern for the poor, powerless, and despised within human society and seeks a more just and compassionate world.

Stewardship

The stewardship testimony acknowledges human destructiveness and the place of humanity within the complex web of life, leading to a desire to live more in harmony with all creation. In effect, this extends the equality testimony to other animals and the rest of the natural world. It both recognizes the increasing power humans exercise over creation and the extent to which human well-being is dependent upon ecological well-being.

Reflecting on Quaker testimony can help prompt people to consider three essential sets of questions about their lives. The first concerns right focus: Are they using their time and giving their attention to the right things? Do their lives reveal a love of God or of some other power? The second refers to right conduct: What does their behavior communicate about their values and motivations? Are they being truthful and honest in all they do, and what impact are they having on others? The final set relates to right relationship: What does their manner of life say about their connections with other people, animals, and the rest of creation? To what extent does it reveal the self-giving love of God and real compassion for their neighbor?

Quaker Testimony Across History

A Radical People (1650–70)

The way that the Quaker movement enacted its testimony during the 1650s gave the impression that it was a serious threat to the established social order. Its witness seemed to disturb dominant social and economic distinctions. In a culture that still assumed that social hierarchies were divinely ordained, some Friends proclaimed that social iniquity was a result of human sin in a fallen world. In the style of the Hebrew prophets, James Nayler condemned economic and social injustice:

> God is against you, you covetous cruel oppressors who grind the faces of the poor and needy . . . and hereby getting great estates in

the world, laying house to house and land to land till there be no place for the poor; and when they are become poor through your deceits then you despise them and exalt yourselves above them.[13]

In a deeply patriarchal society, where women were largely confined to the private sphere as the possessions of men, Friends affirmed the spiritual equality of women living in the new birth, where such divisions are overcome and "all are one in Christ Jesus" (Gal. 3:28). In her tract, *The Just and Equal Balance Discovered* (1660), Sarah Blackborow suggested that "Christ was one in the male and in the female; and as he arises in both."[14] Any attempt to stop a woman from preaching meant silencing Christ, who was speaking through her. In responding to the Pauline injunction that women should remain silent in the church (1 Cor. 14:34-35), Friends argued that since Christ was the bridegroom and the Church was his bride (Rev. 19:7), it was the whole Church, including both men and women, who should keep silent and learn from Christ. In *Women's Speaking Justified* (1665), Margaret Fell wrote:

> Those that speak against the Power of the Lord, and the Spirit of the Lord speaking in a Woman, simply by reason of her Sex, or because she is a Woman, not regarding the Seed, and Spirit, and Power that speaks in her; such speak against Christ and his Church, and are of the Seed of the Serpent.[15]

The experience of Christ dwelling in them and speaking through them was powerfully liberating for ordinary people, and especially for women, who played a full part in public ministry, even if this outraged the wider society. However, these were essentially religious freedoms, and while they appeared to challenge social norms, equality within the spiritual realm did not imply equality within human society. In the context of severe persecution and a struggle for survival, Friends acted to reassure the wider society that they posed no threat to the existing social order, and they came to be perceived as an "innocent and harmless people."[16]

A Peculiar People (1670–1820)

When Friends first emerged, the Quaker movement's sense of being caught up in the unfolding end times seemed to indicate that they were intent on turning the world upside-down, sweeping away the foundations of the existing social order. However, as time went on, it became clear that Quaker testimony primarily reflected their belief that they were the true church, and this made them look peculiar to those around them. Such a sectarian preoccupation remained dominant well into the nineteenth century. The witness of Friends during this time provides a good example of the negative and positive dimensions of Quaker testimony. In negative terms, Friends rejected what they understood to be the corruptions of a dead faith and the fallen ways of the world. In a positive sense, as God's people, they felt they were embodying a true and living faith.

Rejecting the Dead Faith

Much of early Quaker testimony represented a refusal to participate in what Friends regarded as a false and corrupted faith based on the outmoded ways of the old covenant. They associated this most strongly with the Church of England but opposed other expressions of Christianity too. Friends rejected all physical liturgies and sacraments, a set-apart priesthood, the observation of the church calendar, and the belief that there are buildings and land that are especially sacred. In addition, like other nonconformists, Friends withdrew from the parish system and resisted the payment of tithes, which functioned as a tax used to fund the parish institutions. So, while they agreed with all those who sought to end the state-church alliance, their vision was quite distinctive and sectarian.

Embodying the Living Faith

The Quaker rejection of the dominant expressions of Christianity reflected their belief that they had rediscovered the new covenant faith they associated with the apostolic Church. Early Quaker testimony demonstrated how they felt this faith should be practiced. This meant adopting an unprogrammed and spontaneous form of worship, an understanding of ministry as God's direct call discerned by the community, a belief that every day and all times were potentially sacramental and that meeting houses were convenient places for gathering, rather than sacred spaces. In place of the parish system, they established their own arrangements to support traveling ministers and those in need within the community, using voluntary financial contributions.

Rejecting the Ways of the World

The distinction Friends made between the dead faith and the living faith was closely connected to a similar comparison between the fallen ways of the world and the ways of God's people. Their testimony, therefore, rejected any aspect of the dominant culture they considered inconsistent with divine guidance and the true faith. Because only God was worthy of worship, they refused to participate in accepted practices of social deference. Following Jesus's teaching (Mt. 5:33-37), they would not swear oaths. They repudiated violence and fighting with physical weapons because, in the new covenant, God's kingdom could only be realized by inward spiritual struggle. Like other Puritans, they also avoided the vanity associated with flamboyance and ornamentation in clothing and other personal possessions and what they regarded as frivolous recreations such as games, sports, theater, and comedy.

Embodying the Ways of God's People

Quakers assumed that the conduct of God's people, when grounded in divine guidance, would be in stark contrast to the sinful ways of the world. This prompted forms of embodied testimony that often seemed peculiar to those around them. Friends adopted ways of expressing themselves using language that was intentionally plain and straightforward. In the face of powerful social pressures, they endeavored to address all people in a consistent way, regardless of social status, and practiced simplicity and plainness in their apparel and personal possessions. They emphasized the importance of being truthful in all things, especially in matters of money and business. They also identified as a peaceable people, following Jesus's way of nonviolence. Finally, they tried to ensure that worship and spiritual practice were the primary focus of their lives.

Endogamy

Because early Friends viewed themselves as the true church within a corrupted world, much of their testimony at this time was about protecting their purity by maintaining clear boundaries. One notable way they did this was the practice of endogamy, in which marriage was only permitted between those within the community. To "marry out" or to be married by a priest in another church were offenses that could lead to disownment. Such rules seem to be a common feature of other sectarian religious groups of the time.

Quakers and Enslavement

Friends in the Caribbean and North American colonies were actively involved in enslavement, and many Friends elsewhere benefited financially from the slave-based economy of the British Empire. However, from the mid-eighteenth century onward, the Quaker community became increasingly associated with the abolitionist movement, and the rejection of enslavement became a defining feature of their testimony. Chapter 7 examines this issue in more detail.

A Philanthropic People (1820–1920)

By the nineteenth century, many Quakers had become successful businesspeople who increasingly used their wealth to further a variety of philanthropic endeavors. During this period, Friends generally maintained the overall shape of their earlier testimony in a way that continued to mark them out as a peculiar people. However, the influence, first of Evangelicalism and then Liberalism, led to a softening of sectarian boundaries. This made them more willing to collaborate with other Christian groups, particularly on matters of social and political concern. In addition to involvement in improving education and housing conditions, the most significant areas of witness at this time were abolitionism, temperance, penal reform, and mental health reform.

Abolitionism

By the late eighteenth century, Quaker witness against enslavement had shifted beyond a purely internal matter to become a public campaign.[17] As a result, abolitionism began to define Quaker identity. Friends took practical steps to support African Americans. This included making gifts of land, providing employment and education and offering protection against re-enslavement. Some were willing to break the law by helping formerly enslaved people travel to Canada through the "Underground Railroad."[18] Such work intensified after the American Civil War. However, these efforts did not receive universal support. More conservative Friends were cautious about getting involved in worldly affairs. In America, a conflict developed between gradualists and radicals, and many radical abolitionists were either disowned or resigned their membership, leading to the formation of a new Quaker grouping called the "Progressive Friends."[19] The Civil War also presented Friends with a dilemma. There was a significant tension between their testimony against war and their support for abolitionism. Finally, despite this close association with the abolitionist cause, many Friends remained deeply embedded in the colonial economy and were not immune to the racist attitudes that surrounded them.

Temperance

From the beginning, Friends condemned drunkenness and the consumption of strong spirits. However, due to the dangers of unclean water at the time, the use of weaker ale and wine was commonplace. This pro-moderation, anti-strong drink position characterized Quaker attitudes until the nineteenth century, when many became enthusiastic supporters of the temperance movement, which advocated total abstinence from alcohol.[20] As a result, temperance became another defining characteristic of Quaker identity. This testimony influenced Quaker activities in business and philanthropy in a variety of ways. Several British Quaker businesses, such as Cadbury, Fry, and Rowntree, achieved substantial success as chocolate manufacturers. This seems to have been motivated by the production of drinking chocolate as an alternative to alcohol. The wealth accumulated by such businesses was often used for philanthropic purposes. For example, in seeking to address insanitary housing in England, George Cadbury built the model community Bournville, which explicitly excluded the provision of licensed premises.

Penal Reform

The Quaker concern for prison conditions and criminal justice was influenced by their early experiences as a persecuted sect.[21] This sometimes shaped their actions when in positions of authority. William Penn's "holy experiment" in Pennsylvania[22] included a relatively progressive approach to crime and punishment. During the nineteenth century, Friends played a prominent part in campaigns against corporal and capital punishment and insanitary prison conditions. They also promoted the idea that justice should be based on reform and restoration, rather than simply punishment. The world's first penal reform organization, the Philadelphia Society for the Relief of Distressed Prisoners, was established by Friends in 1786. The British Friend, Elizabeth Fry (1780–1845), focused her efforts on improving prison conditions for women and children. This involved working for the separation of male and female prisoners and the use of female wardens. By the end of the century, Quakers were recognized as leaders in this field. Another British Friend, Edward Grubb (1854–1939), supported a focus on rehabilitation and was the secretary of a campaign group that became the Howard League for Penal Reform.

Mental Health Reform

Because of their nonconformity and strongly embodied charismatic behavior, the earliest Friends were often branded as insane and unstable. This may have made them more sensitive than most to the plight of those experiencing mental illness.[23] People suffering in this way were often thought to be demon-possessed and were locked away, treated brutally, and used for public entertainment. During the early part of the nineteenth century, the Quaker Tuke family, of York in England, developed a "moral treatment" of the mentally ill, which replaced coercive control and ridicule with more therapeutic and holistic approaches. They also established The Retreat, an institution that formed the basis of the modern system of mental health hospitals. The Quaker conviction that all people have the capacity for fundamental change may have enabled Friends to become pioneers in the humane treatment of mentally ill people.

A Missional and Campaigning People (1920–Present)

The divisions among Friends that developed during the nineteenth century have, in turn, produced diversity in their testimony. This means that, during the modern period, Quakers have tended to maintain unity on some matters, for example, peacebuilding and opposition to war, while other issues, such as sexuality and gender identity, have become a source of conflict. Evangelical Friends have given significant attention to mission, motivated by the Great

Commission (Mt. 28:16-20), while Liberal Friends have found that their testimony increasingly aligns with contemporary political activism and campaigning.

Mission

Perhaps the most notable aspect of witness among Evangelical Friends has been their strong commitment to international mission and evangelism. The significant success of this work has transformed the Quaker community from a small transatlantic people into an increasingly global community in which most Friends live in the Global South. At the beginning of the twentieth century, three young North American Friends, Arthur Benton Chilson, Willis Hotchkiss, and Edgar T. Hole, began a mission to Kenya which, over time, has produced large numbers of Quakers in East Africa.[24] Shortly after this, further missions focused on Central and South America, resulting in a considerable Quaker presence in the region, particularly in Bolivia.[25] It is hard to overestimate the significance of these developments for the overall size, shape, and orientation of contemporary Quakerism. The communities that emerged out of these Evangelical missions are the ones that continue to grow, when numbers elsewhere are either stagnant or in decline.

War, Peacebuilding, and Disarmament

The early Quaker testimony against fighting with outward weapons has developed into a more general commitment to peace and nonviolence. This has presented Friends with significant challenges and has often placed them at odds with those around them. Such challenges became particularly pressing during the twentieth century, in the context of two world wars, the development of nuclear weapons, and the emergence of the Cold War.[26] In Britain and the United States, the introduction of conscription during the world wars tested Friends' commitment to peace and their relationship with the nation-state. Although Friends as a community held firm to their historic testimony, in practice, Quaker men of fighting age took one of three different paths: some refused any involvement and were imprisoned; others opted for some form of alternative service; and some enlisted. In this situation, Quakers helped secure official recognition of conscientious objection, established forms of alternative service, such as the Friends Ambulance Unit,[27] and campaign groups such as the American Friends Service Committee.[28] Following both world wars, they were actively involved in relief work, supporting those whose lives had been severely disrupted by the conflict. Then, as tensions between East and West deepened, many in the Quaker community became actively involved in the growing peace movement, supporting the Campaign for Nuclear Disarmament and opposing the arms trade. This kind of witness has continued into the early twenty-first century.

As Quakers have become a genuinely global movement, Friends have put their commitment to peace and reconciliation into practice in fresh ways in new locations. Quaker peacebuilding activities in East and Central Africa offer interesting examples to consider.[29] In their Swarthmore Lecture,[30] Esther Mombo and Cecile Nyiramana described Quaker responses during and after serious incidents of violent conflict in Burundi, Democratic Republic of the Congo, Kenya, Uganda, and especially Rwanda, where a genocide took place in 1994.[31] The long-term impact of European colonialism within this region has helped fuel violent conflict by exacerbating ethnic divisions and engendering political instability and economic insecurity. African Friends know that peace is more than the absence of war: it requires justice, reconciliation, healing, and forgiveness. They have employed a range of methods to help foster peace and justice. Conflict management workshops have taught people the skills needed to deal with interpersonal disputes, and mediation practices have been employed. The Alternatives to Violence Project has focused on preventing conflict by promoting a culture of nonviolence. The

Healing and Rebuilding Our Communities initiative has helped people to address wounds and deep traumas, whichever side they were on. The British Quaker project, Turning the Tide, has been used in Africa to develop nonviolent approaches to tackling injustice.[32] For African Friends, all these activities have been explicitly rooted in the nonviolence of Jesus. Mombo and Nyiramana highlight the crucial role that women have played in this work. They offer a number of profiles of notable African Quaker peacebuilders, including Solange Maniraguha, who is a member of the Evangelical Friends Church in Rwanda. She is a peacemaker, a facilitator for Healing and Rebuilding Our Communities, and has made an important contribution to trauma healing among those caught up in the genocide and its aftermath.

Lobbying and Diplomacy

Early Friends became skilled political lobbyists during the campaign for religious toleration. This aspect of their testimony continues in the modern period, taking on new forms in fresh circumstances. This witness has two distinct dimensions: speaking truth to power and speaking truth with power.[33] In the former approach, Friends feel called to express what they believe to be true in words and actions that challenge dominant ideologies and the conduct of governments and institutions. This reflects the prophetic dimension of Quaker testimony. In the latter approach, Friends seek to address these issues through dialogue with those in authority. This represents a more diplomatic approach to Quaker testimony. There are many examples of Quaker diplomacy, including bodies that engage with international organizations and nation-states. The Quaker United Nations Office (QUNO) works with multilateral organizations, government delegations, and nongovernmental organizations. The Quaker Council for European Affairs (QCEA) links with European institutions. In both cases, the aim is to advocate for policies and actions that support peace and justice.

Racism and Civil Rights

Building on previous abolitionist action, many Friends in the twentieth century have contributed to efforts, led by African Americans, to end segregation and the brutal practice of lynching and to secure civil rights in the United States. The African American Friend Bayard Rustin (1912–87) became a significant figure in the civil rights movement, acting as an advisor to Martin Luther King, Junior. He offered King advice on the use of nonviolent resistance.[34] People of Color have not always felt welcome within Quaker communities, and it is clear that their contribution has been underestimated. Recent scholarship has begun to bring this to light.[35] During the post-war period, due to immigration from former colonies, Britain became an increasingly multicultural society. A key legacy of colonialism has been the impact of racism on the social and political life of the country. Some Friends have been involved in resisting this racism, encouraging intercultural and interfaith dialogue, and in opposing far-right political groups. In 2021, Britain Yearly Meeting made a corporate commitment to becoming an anti-racist faith community.

Ecology

Friends have not necessarily been at the cutting edge of modern ecological thinking. However, their traditional vision of building heaven on earth and their focus on seeking to live simply have a distinctly ecological orientation. This has led to a concern for establishing a more harmonious relationship with the rest of creation.[36] As the ecological crisis has deepened, the need to practice stewardship through sustainable ways of living and the importance of creation care have become key aspects of Quaker testimony.

Sexuality and Gender Identity

The issues of human sexuality and gender identity are a source of conflict among Friends today. Most Evangelical Friends are socially conservative, and many view same-sex relationships and gender fluidity as sinful. Despite this, during the modern period, many Quakers have adopted a welcoming and inclusive approach to queer and gender-nonconforming people.[37] The reason for this may have deep roots within the Quaker tradition. In defending the spiritual equality of women, seventeenth-century Friends argued that the transformed life in Christ transcended all outward divisions associated with ethnicity, social status, and sex. In the 1960s, with the publication of a pamphlet called *Towards a Quaker View of Sex*, a group of Liberal Friends in Britain prompted a conversation that questioned narrow traditional definitions of acceptable human sexual activity and opened up space within which new perspectives could be heard.[38] This acted as the catalyst for a process that culminated in the decision made by Britain Yearly Meeting in 2009 to conduct same-sex marriages. Similarly, the issue of gender diversity has a historical dimension. The late eighteenth-century American Quaker preacher, The Public Universal Friend (born Jemima Wilkinson), regarded themself as a genderless evangelist, and they have become a role model for those Friends whose gender identity does not conform to traditional norms.[39] In many Quaker meetings, including socially liberal Conservative and Evangelical communities, transgender and gender-nonconforming people have found a safe and welcoming environment.

Quaker testimony is the physically embodied fruits of inward spiritual guidance. This chapter has demonstrated how such a witness has been revealed in a variety of ways at different times and in different places across Quaker history.

Notes

1 William Penn, *No Cross, No Crown: A Discourse, Showing the Nature and Discipline of the Holy Cross of Christ* (York: Sessions, 1981), 63–4.

2   Paul Buckley, *Quaker Testimony: What We Witness to the World* (Wallingford, PA: Pendle Hill, 2023), 2–6.
3   Loring, *Listening Spirituality*, Volume 2, 112.
4   Rachel Muers, *Testimony: Quakerism and Theological Ethics* (London: SCM Press, 2015), 39.
5   Stuart Masters, "A Glimpse of Heaven on Earth," *Friends Journal*, June, 1 2021, https://www.friendsjournal.org/a-glimpse-of-heaven-on-earth/ (accessed January 21, 2024)
6   Birkel, *Silence and Witness*, 121.
7   Muers, *Testimony*, 54–104.
8   Muers, *Testimony*, 63, 58.
9   The phrase "holy experiment" comes from William Penn's attempts to establish a place of religious toleration in the American colony of Pennsylvania.
10 Walter Wink, *The Powers That Be: Theology for a New Millennium* (New York: Galilee Doubleday, 1999).
11 Britain Yearly Meeting, *Quaker Faith and Practice*, 19.32.
12 Muers, *Testimony*, 104, 146.
13 Nayler and Kuenning, *The Works of James Nayler*, 66–7.
14 Teresa Feroli and Margaret Olofson, eds., *Witness, Warning and Prophecy: Quaker Women's Writings, 1655–1700* (Toronto, ON: Iter Press, 2018), 199.
15 Wallace, *A Sincere and Constant Love*, 65.
16 *A Declaration from the Harmless and Innocent People of God, called Quakers, Against All Plotters and Fighters in the World* (1660).
17 Elizabeth Cazden, "Quakers, Slavery, Anti-slavery, and Race," in Angell and Dandelion, *The Oxford Handbook of Quaker Studies*, 347–62.
18 The Underground Railroad was an organized network of secret routes and safe houses used by fugitive slaves to escape to the abolitionist Northern United States.
19 See, Chuck Fager, *Remaking Friends: How Progressive Friends Changed Quakerism & Helped Save America* (Durham, NC: CreateSpace, 2014).
20 Sabron Reynolds Newton, "Temperance," in *Historical Dictionary of the Friends (Quakers)*, 2nd edition, ed. Margery Post Abbott, Mary

Chijioke, Pink Dandelion, and John William Oliver Jr (Lanham, MD: Scarecrow Press, 2012), 338.

21 Mike Nellis and Maureen Waugh, "Quakers and Penal Reform," in Angell and Dandelion, *The Oxford Handbook of Quaker Studies*, ed. Stephen W. Angell and Pink Dandelion (Oxford: Oxford University Press, 2013), 377–91.

22 William Penn's "Holy Experiment" refers to the founding of Pennsylvania as a government based on religious tolerance and peaceful coexistence.

23 Charles L. Cherry, "Quakers and Asylum Reform," in Angell and Dandelion, *The Oxford Handbook of Quaker Studies*, 392–404.

24 Robert J. Wafula, "Quakers in Africa: History of the Quaker Movement in Africa," in *The Quaker World*, ed. C. Wess Daniels and Rhiannon Grant (Abingdon: Routledge, 2022), 5–15.

25 Emma Condori Mamani, "Quakers in Bolivia: The Beginnings of Bolivian Friends," in Daniels and Grant, *The Quaker World*, 31–7.

26 Lonnie Valentine, "Quakers, War, and Peacemaking," in Angell and Dandelion, *The Oxford Handbook of Quaker Studies*2013), 371–6.

27 Rebecca Wynter, "'Go Anywhere, Do Anything': The Friends Ambulance Unit, 1914–1959," in Daniels and Grant, *The Quaker World*, 502–12.

28 The AFSC was founded in 1917 to work for peace and social justice in the United States and around the world.

29 Esther Mombo and Cecile Nyiramana, *Mending Broken Hearts, Rebuilding Shattered Lives: Quaker Peacemaking in East and Central Africa* (London: Quaker Books, 2016).

30 Since 1908, the Swarthmore Lecture is an annual address given to the Britain Yearly Meeting.

31 During the Rwandan genocide, an estimated 800,000 Tutsi and moderate Hutu were killed, and 2 million refugees fled the country.

32 See Britain Yearly Meeting, "Peacebuilding in East Africa," https://www.quaker.org.uk/our-work/international-work/east-africa (accessed September 17, 2024).

33 "Speaking truth to power" was a term coined by African American Quaker, Bayard Rustin. This means communicating something

forcefully to those in power. To speak truth "with power" implies a more collaborative and diplomatic approach.

34 Carlos Figueroa, "The Political Activist Life of Pragmatic Quaker Bayard T. Rustin," in Daniels and Grant, *The Quaker World*, 307–18.

35 Harold D. Weaver, Paul Kries, and Stephen W. Angell, eds., *Black Fire: African American Quakers on Spirituality and Human Rights* (Philadelphia, PA: Quaker Press of Friends General Conference, 2011). Donna McDaniel and Vanessa Julye, *Fit for Freedom, Not for Friendship: Quakers, African Americans, and the Myth of Racial Justice* (Philadelphia, PA: Quaker Press of Friends General Conference, 2009).

36 Peter G. Brown and Geoffrey Garver, *Right Relationship: Building a Whole Earth Economy* (San Francisco, CA: Berrett-Koehler, 2009).

37 Brian T. Blackmore, "A Short History of Quaker Inclusion of Gay and Lesbian People," in Daniels and Grant, *The Quaker World*, 368–75.

38 Alastair Heron, ed., *Towards A Quaker View of Sex* (London: Quaker Home Service, 1964).

39 Paul B. Moyer, *The Public Universal Friend: Jemima Wilkinson and Religious Enthusiasm in Revolutionary America* (Ithaca, NY: Cornell University Press, 2015).

Part Three

Contribution and Challenges

6

The Quaker Spiritual Journey

This chapter walks through the various stages of a spiritual journey, which, while not universally applied, reflects the general shape and orientation of Quaker spirituality. Along the way, six contemporary Quaker spiritual writers will act as guides: Margery Post Abbott, Sandra Cronk, Douglas Gwyn, Marcelle Martin, Parker J. Palmer, and Lloyd Lee Wilson.

The Inward Work: Being Attentive and Being Guided

Discomfort: Becoming Aware That All Is Not Well

> Awakening to the spiritual journey often begins with some form of longing, sometimes felt as dissatisfaction with the way things are. Longing remains as a strand of the journey even after one finds a connection with God.[1]

The Quaker spiritual journey usually starts with a growing sense of unease or longing. Friends find that questions arise about who they are, what they are doing, how the world works, and their place within it. These questions don't seem to have easy answers. Things that were previously taken for granted are called into question. This situation may emerge for no apparent reason. However, it is often associated with significant life changes: a failed relationship, an experience of being let down by others, dissatisfaction with one's employment, or a general sense of failure. What had been stable, reliable, and safe suddenly becomes precarious, meaningless, and unsatisfactory. A person may find themselves "all at sea." When they experience such an unsettling situation, they may feel inclined to ignore troublesome thoughts and try to get back to normality. They may seek distractions and hope that the crisis will pass, for example, by working harder, resorting to alcohol, or going on holiday. However, the wisdom of the Quaker spiritual heritage suggests that, rather than ignoring one's feelings or seeking distractions, it is important to stop, turn inward, and listen carefully to what is prompting this sense of discomfort. It becomes clear that, however helpful human reason can be, sometimes there is a need to set it aside and sink into silence and stillness.

> The failure of our rational analytical capacities to give answers leads to a place of darkness and then a new way of knowing. In this empty place, we may meet God.[2]

So, the initial doorway that leads to a path to greater spiritual awareness and development is a discomforting and destabilizing experience of unease which, if a person is willing to acknowledge it, prompts them to pay attention to their inward landscape, perhaps for the first time in their life. In this way, Quakers take their first steps on a journey toward a new life and a new creation.

Paying Attention: Heeding the Promptings of Love and Truth

The first step on the Quaker spiritual journey is a willingness to adopt a state of attentiveness, and deep listening, to become aware of what the Light is revealing within. This is easy to describe, but much more difficult to do. All humans are creatures embedded in a particular time, place, and culture. It is not easy to let go of assumptions, preconceptions, and prejudices. When they are still, whose voices do they hear? Maybe they can only hear their own voice or the voices of the dominant culture. The challenge is to listen deeply, to hear the voice of God, of the earth, and of those people who are usually silenced. A few voices can be very loud, whereas others are often unheard. What is needed is a discipline of real surrender and an openness to what might emerge.

> In order to "stand still in the Light" and stop trampling it, we have to humble ourselves, quiet our hearts and minds, wait to feel its infinite love, receive its divine wisdom, and be led into the newness of life.[3]

What makes this particularly difficult is the human tendency to think they are autonomous and in control of their lives. Paying attention to the "still small voice" is most effective when a person has accepted their limitations. Humans are part of a creation that is good and are loved by God, but the world does not revolve around them. They must be able to balance a sense of worth with an attitude of humility and a willingness to surrender themselves to a power that is ultimately beyond all rational conception. An essential paradox of this journey is that, when people give up all their striving and delusions, they can receive a fundamentally new perception. Many firmly held assumptions turn out to be misconceptions, and they melt away, revealing a glimpse of the truth about themselves and about the world.

> The function of contemplation in all its forms is to penetrate illusion and help us to touch reality. Contemplation is difficult for many of us because we have invested so much in illusion.[4]

Once people come to know the power of contemplation, it becomes an essential ongoing discipline, a thread that binds together all the other stages of the Quaker spiritual journey. However, this is rarely a comfortable process. They come face to face with all manner of unpalatable truths and experience a great temptation to turn away.

Diagnosis: Seeing What the Light Reveals

One of the first things Quakers notice when committing themselves to a discipline of paying attention is that what the Light reveals about them and about the world is rarely comforting. For early Friends, this meant a painful realization that they were caught up in sin, understood as a form of spiritual death. Are people willing to receive the Spirit's diagnosis of their ailments, even if this makes them feel upset and defensive? The temptation to ignore uncomfortable truths and hope they go away is understandable, but ignoring these truths only deepens a sense of illusion so that no real progress can be made. A sickness can only be treated and cured when it has been accurately diagnosed. People need to recognize what afflicts them and the wider society.

> There is no moment at which God is not seeking to be in relationship with each of us, speaking the Word which each of us needs to hear most, offering the help which we most need to receive. The only hinderance in this relationship is our own willingness to accept it, to hear God's Word, to receive God fully and openly.[5]

The Spirit's diagnosis offers many things to ponder: Do people recognize their place within the dominant culture and its systems of power? How does this limit their awareness and understanding? If they accept that the world has gone wrong in all sorts of ways, who benefits from this, and who suffers the consequences? Are they working to transform the unjust structures of society or are they upholding them? It is hard to address these questions unless the truth is revealed and clearly seen. The Spirit's diagnosis helps people to see things clearly. Such diagnosis is not about personal guilt or shame. It is about facing the dissonances in human lives and the way they fall short of the fullness of God's love and justice. This helps people to move closer to divine power as the source of abundant life in a new creation. The treatment required to cure an illness can be unpleasant. The medicine may be bitter and hard to take, but this will lead to renewed health and vitality.

Awakening: Gaining a New Vision

By moving beyond denial to honest acceptance, people begin to see with new eyes and act with fresh clarity and purpose. Their growing sensitivity to inward guidance can bring a whole new vision of themselves and the world. This is an experience of awakening, in which the promptings of love and truth offer a new perception. What does it mean to gain such a new vision? People may find themselves reconsidering their relationship with other humans, other creatures, and the rest of the natural world, asking, "do they exist merely to meet human needs?" Quakers believe that all people have an essential worth that is independent of social assumptions. In gaining a new vision, people become increasingly aware of their interconnection and interdependence and recognize that their health and well-being do not depend on their own efforts alone, but also on their relationship with God and all created things. God is their parent, and other people and animals are their siblings. Although human understanding is always located in a particular time, place, and culture, conscious awareness of such limitations helps expand human perception. This is the fruit of contemplation and discernment.

> The Light pierces with total honesty into our behaviors, words and attitudes. This is not an easy thing to experience! In the refiner's fire, metal is purified so that it can be made useful, as a tool or as a sword. The fire of the Light likewise burns away the dross of life—the foolish or harmful things we have done—to reform us closer to the image of God.[6]

This path also leads to a growing sensitivity to suffering and injustice. Becoming tender to the inward guidance of the Spirit fosters a growing sense of compassion, making it harder to ignore the suffering of others. People begin to feel compelled to act on what has been revealed to them.

As we see more clearly the ways in which society perpetuates ignorance and oppression, it becomes painful to continue conforming in the ways we have done before. We see everything in a new light. We see what allows love and truth to flourish and what does not.[7]

The Testing: Being Discerning

Discernment: Sorting and Testing Motivations

A crucial feature of the Quaker spiritual journey, one that provides the essential link between the inward and outward life, is the discipline of discernment, which is about examining inner motivations, distinguishing between true and false leadings, and identifying the right path to follow. This should be a continuous practice for individuals and communities, one that is used at every stage of the journey. Humans are all bubbling pots of feelings and emotions. How do they sift through all this and separate divine promptings of love and truth from other impulses?

> Every action has some motive behind it, some impetus, a force-field out of which it arises. If we do not explore that force we will never act in a transcendent way; we will live our active lives as automatons who move but do not choose.[8]

While the guidance of the Bible and the example of past Friends can help show the way, people must try to face their dilemmas and decisions without preconceptions, accepting that their natural preferences may be misleading. How can they be vigilant about the influence of socialization on their assumptions and intentions? How can they attend to what love requires of them with humility, recognizing that they may get it wrong?

> Learning to separate impulses and feelings from the guidance of the Inward Light is at the core of the discernment that comes with

spiritual maturity. How do I recognize the voice of the Light? What sound does the Spirit make pushing on my heart?[9]

Although individual Friends are encouraged to exercise discernment in all aspects of their lives, it is within community that this discipline reaches its zenith. Friends are unusual in the degree to which they place trust in a collective experience of inward divine guidance. Such an approach presents many challenges; for example, how to guard against false delusions and how to move beyond personal differences in trying to find a common way forward? For Quakers, the approach to making decisions is founded on a steadfast faith in the power of God to gather what is scattered and unify what is divided.

The Outward Work: Being Adventurous and Being Faithful

New Life: Taking a Different Path

Living adventurously and being willing to take a different path can lead to a new way of life based on fresh perceptions, reconciled relationships, and a growing sense of liberation and wholeness. This is a journey that Quakers believe leads them beyond self-centeredness to a broader, more inclusive vision of the world and their place within it. Such a pilgrimage is best followed within community, as a shared lifelong process, rather than a quick fix. Too often, in a culture dominated by individualism, people underestimate the significance of human interdependence. For some people, one momentous life-changing spiritual experience can transform everything. For others, the journey is more leisurely and meandering, with detours along the way. This new way of life may reveal itself in different ways. A Friend might decide to make a career change, get involved in a campaign group, contribute to community-building activities, or stand for public office. At the same time, it may be that their daily activities remain the same, but the way they undertake them changes. This can mean adopting a fresh approach to interpersonal relationships and finding a new sense of purpose. What makes the difference is the Spirit of love and truth becoming the principal motivating force, so that God is visibly at work in human lives.

> With each step we take under divine guidance we become more tested and grounded in the Spirit and can gain spiritual maturity. As we mature, the Seed of Truth and Love grows within our hearts and shapes our behavior. The fruits that come of the Seed is a life which reflects God's Way on earth.[10]

The apostle Paul described the essential characteristics of this new life as the fruits of the Spirit—love, joy, peace, patience, kindness, generosity, faithfulness, gentleness, and self-control (Ga. 5:22-23). Something of the divine nature, however imperfect, is embodied in people's lives, just as it was revealed in fullness in the life of Jesus. When seeking to live in this way, people will often fall short, but if they ignore divine guidance, nothing changes. This is what it means to live adventurously, being willing to take risks and try out new things. It is a two-way process: when someone acts on spiritual guidance, the experience of living their faith in the world will, in turn, have an impact on their inward lives.

> the inner and outward being are integrally related, with the actions and activities of the outward being reflecting the individual's true inward spiritual condition. We also know from personal experience that the relationship works in the other direction as well: what we do outwardly often shapes or changes our spiritual condition.[11]

Testimony: Being Patterns and Examples

The final stage of the Quaker spiritual journey is developing a commitment to being faithful, finding the courage and resolve to act on the inward guidance that has been received and discerned. The visible manifestation of this action in the world is what Friends call testimony. In traditional Quaker spirituality, testimony is understood to have a single consistent source, the way of Christ, made known to people through the promptings of love and truth in their hearts. Friends today see the source of this testimony in more varied ways, but it is always a situated response to particular circumstances at a specific point in time.

> All our practices, all our testimonies flow from the teachings and example of Jesus. Yet they are not simple repetitions of the words and teachings of Jesus, nor is our faith a replication of a 17th-century faith.[12]

The testimony of Friends is not primarily a set of values or ideals; it is an embodied response to inward spiritual guidance. Therefore, a testimony does not exist unless it is being lived. The sense of being inwardly guided prompts people to become "patterns and examples."[13] Being patterns means that their lives take the visible shape of the Spirit of love and truth. Being examples implies that what they do and what they say reach out to others and communicate something about the divine nature and the human capacity to embody it. This assumes that, when guided by God's Spirit, all humans and their social structures can change for the better. What individuals feel called to do is their personal testimony. What the community feels called to do together is corporate testimony. Because the leadings of the Spirit are consistent and unchanging, Friends have found that their testimony over time takes on a definable shape. If they pay careful inward attention and undertake their discernment rigorously, their lives will reflect, in some form, the historic Quaker commitments to nonviolence, truthfulness and integrity, justice, fairness, and compassion. This is an ongoing dynamic process which binds together inward spiritual experiences and outward physical lives.

So the outward practices that form our testimony not only express our inner convictions. They also add further clarity to that conviction. The inward and the outward continue to inform and advance one another as we "live up to the light" we have been given.[14]

Faithfulness: Steadfast Commitment to Love and Truth

Following a leading of any sort generally requires some aspect of self-control, self-denial, or challenge that invites us to "die to ourselves" and live into the ways of God and Christ. Leadings ask us to give our energy and resources to God's projects rather than those of our own devising.[15]

Acting faithfully on guidance received and discerned is not always easy. Being led by the Spirit to interrupt and resist dominant assumptions and ways of living may well bring people into conflict both with the powers that be and with their friends and neighbors. Steadfastly following the way of love and truth often makes Quakers look odd and provokes hostility. They may be misunderstood and misrepresented, face ridicule and even violence. This has been the case, for example, for conscientious objectors during times of war. No one relishes this kind of hardship, but it may be an inevitable consequence of seeking to do what is right. Friends have often understood the cross of Jesus as representing a willingness to surrender one's own desires and preferences in order to do God's will. The desire to avoid discomfort and conflict is one of the great tests of faithfulness. What is clear is that individuals cannot bear this alone; they need the upholding support of a community to help them resist unhelpful social pressures. Not everyone is called to take dramatic and costly actions. For many, what matters most is being faithful in the small everyday things, which can prepare them for more serious and life-changing challenges when they come along. In the Quaker spiritual journey, it is not enough to rely on one's own resources; these must be augmented by the empowerment of the Holy Spirit, which drives out fear and enables people to live adventurously. A willingness to follow divine guidance helps engender a greater sense of empathy and compassion.

> Grasping brings less and letting go brings more . . . we cannot buy the security and identity we seek. Those will come to us only as we let go and live in the grace of God, and in solidarity with those for whom scarcity is not illusion but a matter of life and death.[16]

New Creation: Participating in the Rule of Love and Truth

> Every life is lived towards a horizon, a distant vision of what lies ahead. . . . When we imagine ourselves moving toward the finality of death, our action may become deformed. . . . But when we envision a horizon which holds the hope of life, we are free to act without fear, free to act in truth and love and justice today because those very qualities seem to shape our own destiny.[17]

Across history, Quakers have been inspired and motivated by a vision of a renewed creation, a world under the rule of love, justice, and harmony, rather than hatred, injustice, and destructiveness. They have envisaged a world where humans recognize and celebrate diversity and complexity, live in harmony with the rest of creation, and heal divisions. Experience tells them that, at least for now, in the world as it currently is, they may only get fleeting glimpses of this vision. Hence, the way of being attentive, being guided, being discerning, being adventurous, and being faithful is about following a winding and uncertain pathway full of hope and expectation.

> Recognizing God's presence within and among us, we can be guided by the Light in everything we do. The Eternal Being is knocking upon the heart of each person, waiting to be acknowledged and

welcomed into awareness, wanting to create, through us, heaven on earth.[18]

Perhaps one way of understanding this journey is to see it as a pathway that moves beyond a narrow and self-centered vision to a way of perceiving things from the divine perspective. This, in turn, leads to an experience of love, empathy, and compassion which is equally unconfined. Because this unbounded love and wisdom is available in the Spirit, all can share in it, but only if they are prepared to recognize its presence, accept it, and pay attention to it. This means surrendering a narrow and self-centered point of view and allowing themselves to be reshaped by a bigger, broader, and more inclusive vision. A narrowness of view becomes a deeper, broader perception. Limited experience and understanding become an openness to diversity and complexity. A way of living based on self-centeredness is overcome by a growing sense of compassion and empathy for all things. This is what Quakers believe can be experienced on the pathway to a new creation.

> The choice to live in the end-time, is itself a testimony against those unfaithful structures of our present society. But the choice also recognizes that in the ultimate sense we do not build God's new order. . . . Fundamentally the kingdom is God's gift. We are invited to participate in that new order which is coming and come.[19]

Taking Stock: Evaluating the Experience

Fresh Insights: A Review

The key stages of the Quaker spiritual journey might appear to be a linear process, taking a straight and direct route from the experience of discomfort to the discovery of a new creation. In reality, of course, the way is far more complicated and nuanced. The pathway seems to twist and turn and constantly doubles back on itself. Before the new creation is fully realized for all people and all creatures, it may look more cyclical or spiraling. As people live their lives, they will constantly move through these various stages. Along this path, they will need to maintain an ongoing practice of paying attention to divine guidance and exercising discernment about where it is leading them. Every stage of the process and every circuit of the journey brings fresh revelations and new opportunities for learning, not just from fellow travelers, but also from their own mistakes and obstacles encountered. So, there is a constant need to be taken back to the inward work of being attentive and being guided as the essential root and ground of this spiritual journey. The pathway stretches out before them, and they keep moving on with hope and expectation.

Notes

1 Marcelle Martin, *Our Life Is Love: The Quaker Spiritual Journey* (San Francisco, CA: Inner Light Books, 2016), 16.
2 Sandra Cronk, *Dark Night Journey: Inward Re-patterning Toward a Life Centred in God* (Pendle Hill Publications, 1991), 59.
3 Douglas Gwyn, *A Sustainable Life: Quaker Faith and Practice in the Renewal of Creation* (Philadelphia, PA: Quaker Press of FGC, 2014), 5.
4 Parker J. Palmer, *The Active Life: A Spirituality of Work, Creativity, and Caring* (San Francisco, CA: Jossey Bass, 1999), 25, 27.
5 Wilson, *Gospel Order*, 34.
6 Abbott. *To Be Broken and Tender*, 14–15.
7 Martin, *Our Life Is Love*, 76.
8 Palmer, *The Active Life*, 58.
9 Abbott, *To Be Broken and Tender*, 58.
10 Abbott, *To Be Broken and Tender*, 124.
11 Wilson, *Gospel Order*, 181.
12 Abbott, *To Be Broken and Tender*, 42.

13 A phrase taken from George Fox's letter from Launceston Gaol (Jail) written in 1656.
14 Gwyn, *A Sustainable Life*, 42.
15 Martin, *Our Life Is Love*, 129.
16 Parker J. Palmer, *The Promise of Paradox: A Celebration of Contradictions in the Christian Life* (Notre Dame, IN: Ave Maria Press.1980), 101.
17 Palmer, *The Active Life*, 139.
18 Martin, *Our Life Is Love*, 191.
19 Cronk, *Dark Night Journey*, 28–9.

7

The Critical Friend

Reviewing the Quaker Experience

This final chapter takes a more analytical look at the Quaker way and assesses some of its potential strengths and weaknesses. This includes revisiting the dynamic tensions that present Friends with real challenges in maintaining a balanced faith. It also examines some situations in which Quakers have failed to live up to the high ethical standards they profess. This will include the issues of class and social status, colonialism, enslavement and racism, and the position of women.

The Quaker Way: A Balanced Faith?

The Quaker way is rooted in the experiences and convictions of the first Friends in the seventeenth century. This produced several traditional emphases, including the rejection of outward liturgies, images, and creeds; a suspicion of fixed doctrine and statements of faith; a focus on unmediated spiritual experience; and a sense of caution about human authority, leadership, and hierarchy.

Outward Forms

The earliest Quakers rejected the use of outward liturgies and images, because they believed that such forms tended to distract people from the living presence of God within them. They felt that if God was already present and available, there was no need to focus on mere symbols of this presence. This attitude is understandable in the context of a charismatic revival, but it becomes more challenging during periods of spiritual dryness and inactivity. In such circumstances, liturgy can help a community cope with a sense of divine absence.[1] Pastoral and Evangelical Friends have adapted traditional Quaker practice by programming worship and being more accepting of external imagery. Although Liberal Quakers have maintained unprogrammed worship and tend to avoid religious imagery, some individuals combine this with practices drawn from other traditions that use ritual and symbolism. Conservative Friends feel that these innovations represent a watering down of essential aspects of the Quaker way.

Creeds and Doctrine

The first Friends rejected the credal basis of Christianity and were suspicious of fixed statements of faith. This, again, reflected their focus on a living relationship with God, which they felt could never be adequately codified using human language and reason. What really mattered were the experience of divine intimacy and the impact this had on a person's spiritual state and life within the world. This issue has been at the heart of many disputes and separations within the Quaker community. Some Friends have wanted to avoid statements of faith at all costs, whereas others have worried that a lack of clarity about belief leads inevitably to a drift away from the Christian and biblical foundations of the faith. Pastoral and Evangelical Friends have been more inclined to see the value of statements of faith in providing the community with acceptable boundaries and a clear identity. While both Conservative and Liberal Friends have remained closer to the early Quaker position, the modern practice of listing

Quaker testimonies can sometimes appear to take on a credal dimension.

Unmediated Experience

The first Friends were convinced that life in the new covenant faith was one in which people enjoyed a direct inward relationship with God in Spirit, without the need for physical mediators. This meant that they doubted the value of human traditions and gave absolute priority to divine revelation. The Bible was regarded as an exception, but only when read under the inspiration of the Holy Spirit. Subsequent generations found it difficult to sustain this position in a strict sense. Over time, they became more accepting of tradition, having inherited one of their own. An end-time experience morphed into a mean-time practice in which Friends had to traverse competing sources of inspiration and guidance. Evangelical Friends have placed a degree of trust in the wider Evangelical Christian movement, while Liberal Friends have drawn deeply from a range of multi-faith and secular influences.

Human Authority

Caution about the role of human authority, leadership, and hierarchy has its roots in the early Quaker belief that, in the true faith, people are ruled by God and not by earthly authorities. This was part of their critique of a corrupted Church, which they felt was controlled by men, rather than God. To survive, Friends had to establish communal order and discipline, which inevitably involved an element of human authority, even if the structures they developed were designed to enable the Holy Spirit to guide and lead. A good deal of conflict among Quakers has been focused on disputes about authority, and in particular, who is channeling the divine will and who is asserting their own human motivations.

The Dynamic Tensions

Given the complex mix of characteristics found in the earliest Quaker movement, subsequent generations have had to discern how these should be reflected in their current faith and practice. This dilemma is linked to several dynamic tensions which, while not unique to the Quaker tradition, have proved to be particularly challenging for Friends. The first generation experienced such an intense sense of divine encounter that external sources of spiritual support and guidance seemed redundant. Living in a state of perpetual spiritual baptism, combined with an ongoing sense of communion with God, were interpreted as signs of the end times. But what happens to this kind of community when the charismatic fires die down and the expected kingdom of God does not arrive? How is an end-time spirituality sustained in the meantime? The following analysis considers eight dynamic tensions which reveal the nature of this challenge.

God's Kingdom and the World

Friends have found themselves caught between the world as it is and the vision of a new creation revealed to them by God. This has created a dynamic tension between two distinct influences: the ways of God's kingdom and the ways of the world. Friends have had to decide whether they wish to be a peculiar people, separated from their neighbors, or a community fully involved in society. During the first two centuries, they found a way to be spiritually separated from the world, while yet actively engaged with it. Once Quaker sectarianism began to break down in the nineteenth century, Friends have increasingly absorbed and reflected the culture that surrounds them. A majority moved in an Evangelical direction within the culture of nineteenth-century Britain and America. Finding themselves in increasingly liberal and multicultural societies during the past hundred years, some

Friends have become Liberal and pluralist in outlook. Depending on one's perspective, this protean quality can be viewed positively or negatively. On the one hand, it means that, in each generation, the Quaker faith maintains its relevance by adapting to its time and place. On the other hand, some worry that Friends are too easily influenced and lack sufficient independence and rootedness. However, the lines of influence can travel in both directions; Quakers may well have played a part in shaping the dominant culture. What seems clear is that a community which is aware of the factors influencing it is better placed to undertake effective discernment.

Revelation and Tradition

Friends have always practiced an experiential and Spirit-led faith based on continuing revelation, making them suspicious of the traditions of the Church. But since the seventeenth century, all Quakers have inherited a preexisting tradition of their own. This has engendered a dynamic tension between the spiritual guidance they receive in the present and the tradition they have inherited from the past. In his *Journal*, George Fox claimed that his understanding of the true faith came "in the pure openings of the Light without the help of any man,"[2] but it is clear that early Quaker ways closely reflected a radical form of Puritanism that had already existed in England for around three decades. So, the faith of Friends has always been a mixture of tradition and fresh revelation. All the diverse expressions of Quakerism today recognize the authority of early Friends but interpret them in quite different ways. For Evangelicals, George Fox and other early leaders were examples of an emerging Evangelical Christianity. For Liberals, on the other hand, they are viewed as mystical universalists whose Christian and biblical worldviews were incidental features of their religious context. In various ways, Friends have tried to balance the competing demands of their tradition and the experience of fresh revelation. This is never easy, but good discernment plays an important role in ensuring that the community doesn't just replicate the past nor simply reflect the dominant culture of the day.

Christian and Universal

The early Quaker movement represented a peculiarly universalist understanding of the Christian faith. Early Friends regarded themselves as the one true church, but they also believed in a universal church of the Spirit which, for individuals, was unconstrained by time, place, culture, and external religious observance. This combination of Christian exclusivism and spiritual universalism has developed in quite different ways over time, meaning that a rather small group now holds within it a significant diversity of belief and practice. At one pole, some Friends within the more conservative Evangelical Friends Churches feel sympathy for Christian fundamentalism. At the opposite pole, many Friends within Liberal Quaker meetings are pluralists, humanists, and atheists. Evangelical Friends have sat lightly on the universalist dimensions of their Quaker heritage, while emphasizing their Christian and biblical roots. A key challenge for Evangelical Friends is finding ways to balance their Evangelical identity with traditional Quaker peculiarities. Liberal Friends have tended to play down the explicitly Christian roots of their heritage, while emphasizing its universalist dimensions. A key challenge for Liberal Friends is balancing their preference for pluralism and universalism with the biblical origins of the Quaker tradition. This raises a key question—is the Quaker way essentially a distinctive expression of Christianity or a more universalist practice open to people of all faiths and none?

Divine Sovereignty and Human Action

There is a dynamic tension within Quaker spirituality between a quietist inward practice of surrender before God and a lived faith of embodied human action. Early Friends believed that all human conduct, whether spoken, written, or enacted, should be a faithful response to God's guidance, in which their own motivations played no part. As their early sense of spiritual empowerment began to wane, Friends were less likely to enact charismatic and embodied responses. This raised important questions for them. If they were no longer regularly experiencing a prophetic call, was this because God had fallen silent or was it because they were failing to hear the divine voice? In such circumstances, Friends became increasingly suspicious of their motivations, leading to a greater preoccupation with discernment. Over time, Quakers have relaxed this approach to some extent. In both the Evangelical and Liberal expressions of the Quaker way, Friends accept that people must take responsibility for their actions and can interrogate and test their motivations. For example, when Friends come together for worship, listen for divine guidance, and exercise discernment, this involves a degree of intentionality which implies both spiritual surrender and active agency. A careful balance is required because extreme forms of passivity and surrender can lead to a neglect of individual and collective accountability, whereas an overemphasis on human autonomy and control detracts from the centrality of divine guidance and underestimates human limitations.

Inwardly Quiet and Emotionally Expressive

Friends have found it hard to hold together two essential aspects of the early Quaker movement: the quiet inward approach to worship and spiritual practice, and the strongly charismatic and expressive response. Unprogrammed Friends in the Conservative and Liberal traditions have tended to emphasize the former, while Pastoral and Evangelical Friends have recovered aspects of the latter. Few contemporary Friends have been able to replicate the combination visible in the first generation. The period stretching from the late seventeenth to the early nineteenth century has sometimes been called "Quietist," reflecting the decline of charismatic fervor and the dominance of quiet inwardness. During the nineteenth century, it is said that many young Friends found the silence of unprogrammed worship lacking in vitality and were attracted to the exuberant and expressive faith associated with the Evangelical revivals. At the beginning of the twentieth century, there were many interesting interconnections between Evangelical Friends and the emerging Pentecostal movement. For example, Ambrose Jessup Tomlinson (1865–1943), coming out of the Quaker community in Indiana, was a founder of the Pentecostal, Church of God of Prophecy. However, Evangelical Friends were not willing to fully embrace the Pentecostal understanding of the gifts of the Holy Spirit, and those who wished to move in that direction either left or were disowned. John Wimber, who established the Vineyard Church, left an Evangelical Friends Church in California. Within modern Liberal Quaker communities, this tension is often reflected in a distinction between spiritual Friends and social activists. This raises another key question—is the Quaker way essentially a quiet and contemplative tradition, or an embodied charismatic faith?

Spiritual Freedom and Communal Order

There is a dynamic tension within the Quaker way between the spiritual freedom of individuals to follow their own leadings and the need for an ordered community with discernible boundaries and a clear identity. Again, an appropriate balance is not easily maintained. During some periods, corporate order and control have severely limited personal freedom. Today, a more permissive culture has come to predominate. The earliest Friends rejected what they perceived to be the illegitimate power of the established Church and proclaimed that Christ had come to teach his people himself. This seemed to prioritize direct personal experience over the authority of any institution. As a result, Quakers have often been portrayed as individualists. However, as it struggled to survive persecution, the Quaker movement transformed itself into a highly ordered and disciplined community. The desire to protect their perceived status as the true Church led to rigorous enforcement of discipline in which corporate order took precedence over individual freedom. Today, particularly in its more Liberal form, Quakers often promote themselves as a community where everyone is free to follow their personal spiritual journeys. At a time when many are skeptical of organized religion, Liberal Quakerism may appeal to those who regard themselves as "spiritual but not religious."[3] Is it possible for Friends to steer a course between the extremes of authoritarian institutional control and the fragmentation of radical individualism?

Divine Perfection and Human Fallibility

The earliest Friends took the reality of evil very seriously, but they also believed that God could liberate them from sin in this life. This created a dynamic tension between human fallibility and the possibility of perfection. In Quaker spirituality, holiness and perfection are regarded as divine characteristics which can be revealed in the lives of faithful people. Liberal Friends tend to view a preoccupation with sin as anachronistic, preferring to emphasize the essential good in all people. However, without a conception of sin, it is hard to offer an adequate spiritual explanation for the reality of human violence, injustice, and destructiveness. Evangelical Friends place sin and salvation at the center of their faith, but some are inclined to understand sin primarily in personal terms and may neglect the significance of the structural sources of evil. How a faith community defines what is good and healthy and what is destructive and evil is an important matter for discernment. Evangelicals will want to appeal to the Bible, whereas Liberals will be more inclined to draw on modern psychology and sociology. Both will pay some attention to the wisdom and witness of earlier Friends. In terms of achieving a balance within this tension, too much emphasis on holiness and perfection may be unrealistic, leading to spiritual conceit and legalism, while too much emphasis on human goodness may be naïve, acting as a justification for self-centered and unethical behavior.

Free Ministry and Employed Staff

The conviction that ministry should be freely offered was a key aspect of early Quaker testimony. However, from the beginning, Friends were willing to appoint employees to undertake administrative functions. In England, Ellis Hookes was employed as a paid clerk in 1657. While Conservative and Liberal Quakers have continued to undertake all key spiritual roles on a voluntary basis, since the late nineteenth century, Pastoral and Evangelical Friends have appointed paid pastors to act as released ministers. This reflects a dynamic tension between paid and unpaid roles within Quaker communities that has had a number of implications. The rejection of a set-apart paid clergy enabled Friends to maintain structures that avoided fixed hierarchy, offering a range of opportunities for members to give service based on their discerned gifts. However, the commitment to unpaid roles has tended to favor those who have either the wealth or the time needed to offer such service. Key roles may be dominated by those who have retired from paid employment, limiting the opportunities available to younger Friends, particularly parents with young children. In addition, with declining numbers and increasing busyness in modern life, it is sometimes difficult to fill vacant roles. The use of paid pastors within Pastoral and Evangelical Quaker communities helps ensure that key functions are undertaken, while still retaining voluntary roles. It is important to emphasize that Quaker pastors are people with a discerned gift for ministry who are enabled ("released") to exercise this ministry within the community. Again, this leads to a question of balance. A faith community that relies too heavily on hierarchical structures and an employed ministry may disempower its membership, giving too much authority to the few. A faith community that relies on unpaid volunteers may struggle to fill positions and provide role holders with the kind of training needed to undertake their work effectively.

Rebellious and Respectable

At the beginning, Friends were regarded as a highly disruptive presence, challenging the established Church and the secular authorities with messages of warning and denunciation that reflected the actions of the Hebrew prophets. However, within a short period of time, they became a peaceable people who, while appearing peculiar, were increasingly wealthy and respectable. This has created a dynamic tension between the prophetic impulse to be a rebellious people and the desire to be a well-respected community. Throughout most of their history, Friends have tended to emphasize the respectable over the rebellious, and they have often condemned and disowned the prophets within their midst. Nevertheless, such prophets have continued to emerge in each generation, seeking to appeal to the Quaker conscience.

The Quaker way functions best when it achieves some sort of balance between these dynamic tensions. However, there will always be disagreements about exactly where this balance should be. Some Friends will have a clear preference for one end of the tension over the other, reflecting their personal preferences and their theological orientation.

Discomforting Aspects of Quaker History

When it comes to exploring situations in which Quakers have got things wrong, it is important to recognize that such assessments are inevitably made with the benefit of hindsight, through the retrospective lens of current cultural norms, and within a specific social context.

It may be equally hard for people today to recognize their mistakes and limitations clearly and objectively. That said, there have been a number of issues that appear to be contrary to the professed values of Friends.[4] It may be helpful to first set the scene by revisiting the major changes that took place within the movement during its first thirty years. Intense persecution led to a struggle for survival in which Friends decided to safeguard their spiritual peculiarities at all costs, while suppressing social and political ideas that might appear threatening to the existing social order. As a result, the Quaker community managed to survive, becoming increasingly wealthy and respectable in the process. This created two dynamic tensions that are pertinent in making sense of the more discomforting aspects of Quaker history. The first is the balance between God's guidance and the influence of the world. The other is the way Quakers have identified themselves as both rebellious and respectable. It seems that Quakers have tended to err when the ways of the world and the desire for respectability have been dominant.

Class and Social Status

The early Quaker rejection of established practices of social deference gave the impression that Friends were intent on eradicating social inequality, and it is true that some in the first generation, like James Nayler, seem to have been influenced by the social and economic radicalism of the Levellers and the Diggers. However, most Friends were of the "middling sort,"[5] with some members of the gentry, like Margaret Fell, being influential within the movement from the beginning. Quite quickly, leading Quakers were at pains to reassure those in power about their intentions. When a large group of elders met at Balby in 1656, they wrote an epistle advising, "that servants be obedient to them that are their masters in the flesh" (Eph. 6:5). Their spiritual vision may have been egalitarian, but this did not necessarily extend to external forms of social stratification. Having separated themselves from the Church of England, Friends developed a method of poverty relief like the existing parish system, and this prompted them to develop formal membership arrangements to control who was eligible for assistance. These developments coincided with a significant change in the social profile of Friends, with a new generation of leaders, such as Robert Barclay and William Penn, being of high social rank. By the end of the seventeenth century, some Friends were wealthy businesspeople and landowners. This inevitably had an impact on their social attitudes, including how they viewed people of lower rank. The evidence suggests that in the eighteenth century some Quakers regarded servants and the poor as potential corruptors of their children. In her autobiography, Mary Anne Schimmelpenninck (1778–1856), a member of the Quaker Galton family, described how she was discouraged from associating with servants:

> My dear mother, in her scrupulous care, wished to insure that her children should never by any means hold intercourse with servants. . . . She took the greatest pains that we should receive no contamination from ignoble minds, no vulgarism of habits or ideas.

In the nineteenth century, many Quakers were reaching out to the poor in terms of philanthropy and evangelism. They played an important part in the adult school movement which offered working-class men teaching in reading, writing, and Bible study. However, the idea that such people might become members was controversial. The influential British Friend Robert Barclay (1833–76) published a paper in 1870 in which he argued that, while working men might be of equal value before God, this did not mean that Quakers should associate with them socially. He warned that they might become a financial burden on the Society:

Do you wish to invite chimney-sweepers, costermongers, or even blacksmiths, to dinner on First Day? Do you intend to give their sons and daughters a boarding-school education? Do you intend to save the country the expense of supporting them when out of work?

These views may not have been entirely representative, but they do provide some insight into how issues of social status and class played out within Quaker culture. There is evidence that Friends viewed themselves as something of a spiritual elite. In places where the adult schools were active, separate opportunities for worship were established to cater for working-class folk, modeled on the kind of worship common in other nonconformist denominations.

Their commercial success made Quaker businesspeople substantial employers, and this inevitably gave them power over their employees. Although Friends gained a reputation as enlightened and responsible employers, this was not always the case. For example, the Quaker business Bryant and May, who made matches, earned notoriety within trade union history because of the matchgirls' strike of 1888.[6] This strike was a response to extremely poor working conditions, including exposure to white phosphorous, which could have a devastating effect on the health of employees. The action was ultimately successful in securing workplace improvements and led to the formation of the Union of Women Matchmakers.

The past hundred years have seen a major shift in the social profile of Friends. An intermarried group led by wealthy businesspeople has morphed into a community of people joining from outside, often dominated by university-educated professionals who tend to work within white collar roles in the public and charitable sectors. Quaker culture in the West tends to remain very white and relatively affluent and may feel less than attractive to people from other backgrounds. Evangelical Quakers in North America have bucked this trend to some extent, because Friends Churches are often local community churches, drawing a more representative membership from their locality. The issue of class is now being actively discussed by Quakers, particularly in the context of declining numbers. Is it possible for Friends to attract a broader range of people, or will they remain a relatively homogeneous community?

Colonialism, Enslavement, and Racism

Like other dissenters, many Friends found a degree of religious toleration in the British colonies of the Caribbean and North America. When George Fox was first exposed to the harsh reality of enslavement in Barbados in 1671, he faced a serious dilemma. Quakers proclaimed that they were liberated from the evils of a fallen world, but some Friends were already fully engaged in a slave-based economic system; indeed, his stepdaughter, Margaret Fell, Junior, had married into the Rous family, who owned a plantation and enslaved people in Barbados. At the same time, Friends were being accused by those in authority of encouraging enslaved people to revolt. In this situation, Fox sought to articulate a position that reassured those in power, safeguarded the financial interests of individual Friends, and upheld Quaker spiritual principles. Drawing on the Bible, he advocated a practice of enslavement that he felt was appropriate for God's people. In essence, this meant softening some of the more brutal aspects of the system and fully incorporating enslaved people into Quaker families and their worship.[7] It is, perhaps, telling that Fox developed these ideas while staying at the Rous residence in Barbados. Fox's pragmatism and genius for organization have often been celebrated by his admirers, but in this case his actions had far-reaching consequences, which would become deeply discomforting to future generations. As Elizabeth Cazden has concluded, "he determined that it was more important to establish Friends as respectable law-abiding citizens—with submissive law-abiding slaves—than to challenge the system of chattel slavery."[8] As Friends became increasingly wealthy, their economic success enabled them to be investors, landowners, and enslavers. Although there were always individuals and small groups of Friends who opposed enslavement, such as the authors of the 1688 Germantown petition in Pennsylvania, and the early abolitionist, Benjamin Lay,[9] the Quaker community did not begin to withdraw from the practice until the latter part of the eighteenth century, influenced by the testimony of figures such as John Woolman and Anthony Benezet. It then took many decades for all the people enslaved by Friends to be freed. This commitment to abolitionism did not necessarily mean that Friends were united in a broader commitment to racial justice. In America, many remained supportive of racial segregation and opposed Black voting and intermarriage.[10] It was not unusual for meetings to require Friends of Color to occupy segregated seating. This engendered a culture in which African Americans rarely felt fully welcome within Quaker communities, being regarded as "fit for freedom, not for friendship."[11] Despite its global expansion during the twentieth century, the demographic of the Quaker community in the West has remained overwhelmingly White and European in origin, and much of the money that funds its life and work is tainted by past injustices. Friends of Color have described their struggles and frustrations in trying to get their communities to face up to this history and recognize the continued existence of racism within Quaker culture. Like the prophets of the past, those who seek to disturb complacency in pursuit of truth and justice often find themselves labeled as troublemakers, isolated, and sometimes disowned. This, perhaps, reflects an all-too-human desire to maintain peace within the community at the expense of seeking justice. Many yearly meetings are now making significant efforts to address these issues, but there is much left to do.

The Position of Women

In many ways, the position of women within the Quaker community has been one of its strengths. Friends recognized the validity of women's ministry from the beginning of the movement. However, this did not necessarily imply social equality.[12] During the earliest years, women played a full and visible part in Quaker missions as traveling ministers, preachers, and writers. The sight of assertive women preaching in public was viewed as scandalous and an illegitimate encroachment on the male domain. In responding to persecution, Quakers maintained their commitment to the ministry of women, but their freedom became more curtailed. They increasingly came under the oversight of male elders; their more assertive prophetic messages were discouraged; and their efforts were directed toward separate women's business meetings, focusing on more appropriately feminine concerns. There is evidence to suggest that women were more likely than men to be disciplined for inappropriate conduct, reflecting the persistence of traditional gender attitudes within a community seeking to manage its public reputation.[13] Through their yearly meeting structures, male Friends maintained control of decision-making on matters of discipline, doctrine, and political engagement, and it wasn't until the end of the nineteenth century that women began to enjoy equal participation in this work. Women were sometimes excluded from public campaigning on social issues, such as the abolition of enslavement, and Friends were divided on the issue of women's suffrage. Sometimes, Quaker dress regulations could have a negative impact on women. Traditionally, Quaker women wore bonnets, and some designs obscured the woman's face and limited her range of vision. Initially, where paid pastors were introduced, the opportunities for women to exercise ministry declined. When the Quaker community grew in East Africa, Friends challenged some traditional local practices disadvantaging women, but men dominated leadership positions within yearly meeting structures.[14] So, although Friends have had a more positive attitude toward the role of women than many other Christian groups, pressure to conform to dominant social norms has sometimes impacted negatively on their freedom and opportunities.

The fact that Friends have sometimes failed to meet their professed ethical standards need not undermine the essential value and validity of the Quaker way. Those who seek to follow this path are ordinary human beings shaped by a range of physical, psychological, and social limitations. Maintaining a strong sense of self-awareness and humility, along with a serious commitment to the disciplines of spiritual attentiveness and discernment, can help guard against hypocrisy and error.

Notes

1 David L. Johns, *Quakering Theology: Essays on Worship, Tradition and Christian Faith* (Farnham: Ashgate Publishing Limited, 2013), 17–26.
2 Fox, *Journal*, 33.
3 The term "spiritual but not religious" describes people who value a spiritual dimension in their lives but reject the need for institutional religious communities.
4 The material in this section draws on the work of British Friend, Kathleen Bell, during her Eva Koch Scholarship at Woodbrooke Quaker Study Centre in 2019.
5 The "middling sort" included a diverse range of people such as farmers, artisans, and those who worked in business or the professions.
6 Louise Raw *Striking a Light: The Bryant and May Matchwomen and their Place in History* (London: Continuum, 2011).
7 Richard C. Allen, "Beyond Britain: The Quakers in the European Continent and the Americas, 1666–1682," in *The Quakers 1656–1723:*

The Evolution of an Alternative Community (University Park, PA: The Pennsylvania State University Press, 2018), 104–12.

8 Elizabeth Cazden, "'Within the Bounds of Their Consciences' The Testimony of Inequality Among Eighteenth-Century New England Friends," in *Quakerism in the Atlantic World, 1690–1830*, ed. Robynne Rogers Healey (University Park, PA: The Pennsylvania State University Press, 2021), 58.

9 Marcus Rediker, *The Fearless Benjamin Lay: The Quaker Dwarf Who Became the First Revolutionary Abolitionist* (Boston, MA: Beacon Press, 2017).

10 Cazden, "Quakers, Slavery, Anti-slavery, and Race," 357.

11 McDaniel and Julye, *Fit for Freedom*.

12 Margaret Bacon Hope and Pam Lunn, "Women's Issues: Europe and North America," in *Historical Dictionary of the Friends (Quakers)*, 2nd edition, ed. Margery Post Abbott, Mary Ellen Chijioke, Pink Dandelion, and John William Oliver, Jr. (Lanham, MD: Scarecrow Press, 2012), 371–2.

13 Moore, *The Light in their Consciences*, 135.

14 Esther Mombo, "Women's Issues: East Africa," in Abbott et al., *Historical Dictionary of the Friends (Quakers)*, 369–70.

Epilogue

New social, political, and religious movements emerge within unique sets of circumstances and are often shaped by three basic factors: what their members reject as fundamental wrongs, what they affirm as essential truths, and what they have experienced in their own lives. These factors give such movements their power and energy, but they also set their limitations and boundaries. It seems that the early Quaker movement was no exception. It emerged within a period of great turmoil and social change. Like other religious reformers and radicals, Friends rejected Catholic Christendom, which they associated with a corrupted Christianity, in favor of what they regarded as the authentic faith practiced by the early Church. However, they also rejected key aspects of the Reformed Protestant position that was dominant within their time, because it seemed to imply that an unbreachable chasm separated God and humanity, precluding any possibility of experiencing genuine divine intimacy and personal transformation in this life. Instead, Quakers affirmed that, because the Holy Spirit was universally available, all people could enjoy a direct and intimate inward relationship with God and that this would lead to a new birth into the way, the truth, and the life of Christ. This was founded not on the intentional construction of a new set of doctrines and practices but on a response to life-changing spiritual experiences. Crucially, the first Friends found that their spiritual breakthrough came when all social, economic, and religious structures and supports had fallen away and they were forced to rely on God alone. This experience is at the heart of the Quaker rejection of outward forms and mediators in the spiritual life, a principle which can be illustrated using the metaphor of a romantic human relationship. When a couple are living apart, they must rely on indirect ways of remaining connected. This might include the use of photographs, letters, and telephone calls. However, when they can be together in the same physical space, such methods of connection are no longer required.¹ Although over time, Friends' attempts to maintain a single focus on divine intimacy and guidance changed and diversified, each of its different expressions share a spirituality with a recognizable shape and orientation. The Quaker faith has sometimes been called a listening spirituality, but in a holistic sense it might be more accurately described as a listening, hearing, discerning, and obeying spirituality. The inward work of being attentive to the divine presence and experiencing a sense of being guided by God demands careful testing through the discipline of being discerning, leading to the outward work of responding to the divine command by being adventurous and being faithful. It is this binding together of inward spiritual experience, discernment, and embodied action that gives the Quaker way its distinctive character, regardless of its apparent divisions and diversity.

Who Are the Quakers?

If someone enquires about the Quaker faith and what it means, Friends are inclined to describe the version they know best. However, a full and truthful answer will not be simple or straightforward. This is because, within the world today, Friends exist in several quite distinct and divergent forms: Conservative, Evangelical, Pastoral, Liberal, and Pluralist. Despite this complexity, it is possible to identify three broad strands. The first strand views Quakers as the principal representatives of primitive Christianity revived, a recovery of the essential features and practices of the first-century Church, before the development of fixed institutional structures and hierarchy, and the formation of the New Testament. In this understanding, Quakers see themselves as the faithful remnant of true Christianity, and as a peculiar people within the world. Such a view may be held by Conservative Friends, along with some within Evangelical, Pastoral, and Liberal Quaker communities. What matters most here is the preservation of those characteristics that make Friends unique and distinguish them from other Christians. The second strand takes a more ecumenical position, viewing Friends as a distinctive expression of Protestant Christianity and a member of the global Church. In this case, while Quaker peculiarities are cherished, they tend to be viewed as one contribution to the richness and diversity of the Church. Friends can see the value in other forms of Christianity but feel that they have something unique to offer. This attitude can be seen within many modern Evangelical, Pastoral, and Liberal Quaker communities. In the final strand, the Quaker way tends to be regarded as a universal and pluralist spiritual pathway open to all, whose Christian and biblical roots were a logical but inessential reflection of the early movement's religious context. From this position, Quaker practices and processes offer an enabling framework, within which individuals and communities can follow their diverse spiritual journeys regardless of professed belief or modes of expression. This understanding has become dominant in many modern Liberal and Pluralist Quaker communities located within increasingly secular and multi-faith societies, based on an aspiration that the Quaker way has the capacity to unite people of all faiths and none.

What Do Quakers Have to Offer?

What does the Quaker way have to offer the Christian Church and the wider world? At the end of his book *The People Called Quakers*, American Friend Elton Trueblood argues that Quakerism is at its best when it faithfully puts into practice its distinctive gifts, something like a religious order. "An order, though it is not the Church, exists to serve the Church. Its purpose is to produce something which otherwise might be forgotten, lost, or minimized."[2] Maybe this is what God has called Friends to do. Here is a simple list of some of the gifts that Friends might bring to the table:

1. A contemplative spirituality, founded on a practice of "waiting on the Lord" that is unusual within the Protestant wing of Western Christianity. Such a discipline of group listening in silence is rarely seen outside of the monastic orders.
2. A Spirit-led tradition that endeavors to give full attention to the living presence of the Holy Spirit, which has often been neglected and undervalued within Western Christianity. This connects Friends with other charismatic expressions of the faith.
3. Friends have attempted to maintain a "doing it all together" way of organizing the faith community rather than the "doing it for you" or "doing it to you" approaches common in more hierarchical structures. This is reflected in a broad and relatively inclusive view of ministry, which has always recognized the ministry of women.
4. A movement that has aspired to uphold the spiritual seriousness of the monastic orders within day-to-day life in the world. This means combining inward and contemplative spiritual practices with an embodied life of holiness.
5. A unique way of making decisions in worship that aims to achieve unity rather than majority rule through voting. In this discipline, the gathered community as the body of Christ seeks to discern collectively what their head is directing them to do. This seems to reflect the process adopted by the apostles at the Council of Jerusalem (Acts 15).

6. Based on its understanding of the way of Jesus, a tradition that has tried to place nonviolence, peacebuilding, and the pursuit of social justice at the center of its faith and practice.
7. In its Pluralist Liberal form, being a spiritual path offering an open and inclusive faith that seems in keeping with many modern secular societies that are both multicultural and multifaith in nature.

In all these ways and more, Friends have the potential to offer something distinctive and valuable within the world today even if, in practice, they have not always lived up to the values and ideals they profess.

Do Quakers Have a Future?

Across history, compared with other denominations, the Quaker community has remained relatively small. It has rarely been able to attract a mass membership that is representative of the wider society. This may well be due to its religious peculiarities and preexisting social profile. Such a situation seems to support the view that the Quaker vocation is to be a religious order, offering its unique gifts and contributions, but this sits uncomfortably with the traditional claim that the faith of Friends is primitive Christianity revived, the authentic expression of the way of Jesus in the world. Based simply on the current geographical distribution, the prospects for Quakers in the future will depend to a significant extent on developments among Evangelical Friends in the Global South. How will they seek to balance their Quaker convictions with a broader commitment to Evangelical Christianity? To what extent will they continue to develop a Quakerism that differentiates itself from the faith and practice brought by North American missionaries? What other influences, such as postcolonial and liberation theologies, might shape their religious vision? As a much smaller but nevertheless significant group, Liberal and Pluralist Quaker communities face a quite different set of questions and dilemmas. They tend to exist within largely secular societies where religion is increasingly viewed with suspicion and hostility. To what extent can this expression of Quakerism function effectively when separated from its Christian roots? Will the attempt to attract those who see themselves as spiritual but not religious be successful? Can these Friends expand their reach beyond their predominant demographic, which is overwhelmingly White, relatively affluent, and politically Liberal? Finally, while Conservative Friends and others who are strongly committed to preserving the original features of the early Quaker faith are perhaps the smallest grouping within the modern world, they may be best placed to communicate the unique and distinctive Quaker way of being Christian and have a rich and fascinating spirituality to share with the world.

At this point in history, humans are faced with quite unprecedented risks and challenges. For the first time ever, the species genuinely has the capacity to destroy not only itself but also most of the other life forms on earth. This gathering crisis, associated with military power and the dangers of war, ecological destruction, and the threat of climate change, has complex social, political, and economic dimensions. However, at root, it might be best viewed as essentially a spiritual crisis. Why does the human species appear to be so dysfunctional and self-destructive? What would it take for these maladies to be diagnosed, treated, and healed? Perhaps only a fundamental transformation of human nature and being will suffice. What would it take for humanity to achieve right relationship with God, with itself, with other animals, and with the rest of the natural world? Because the Quaker movement emerged out of an earlier time of profound crisis and upheaval and is in essence an end-time spirituality, it might still have something crucial to offer a humanity faced with such significant existential threats. Radical movements of the Spirit like the Quakers may be the Braxton-Hicks of the kingdom of God. In pregnancy, Braxton-Hicks are the initial testing contractions that help prepare the body for full labor and birth. To date, such movements have not succeeded in giving birth to heaven on earth. However, they have anticipated the coming of the kingdom and prepared the world for the birth of a new creation. Whether Friends continue to exist or not, being the Braxton-Hicks of the coming kingdom of God would be a worthy legacy.

Notes

1 Jack L. Willcuts, *Why Friends Are Friends: Some Quaker Core Convictions Practice* (Newberg, OR: Barclay Press, 1984), 38.
2 D. Elton Trueblood, *The People Called Quakers: The Enduring Influence of a Way of Life and a Way of Thought* (New York: Harper & Row, 1966), 283.

Glossary

Theological Terms

Apocalypse/Apocalyptic The revelation of divine mysteries, particularly as they relate to God's ultimate plan for all things.
Charismatics Christians who follow a Spirit-led faith associated with an embodied expression of the gifts of the Holy Spirit, often including speaking in tongues.
Covenant The shape and nature of a relationship between God and humanity, implying specific mutual responsibilities.
Creed/Credal A formal statement of belief that seeks to summarize the essential convictions of a faith.
End times/Eschatology The time when God's plan for all things reaches its fulfillment.
Holiness A way of being human that is aligned to God's will and that reveals the divine nature.
Incarnation God becoming human in Jesus Christ.
Justification The event or process by which humans are made or declared to be righteous in the sight of God.
Liturgical Calendar The cycle of seasons and holy days that form the structure of the Church year.
Mysticism A spirituality emphasizing inward spiritual experience, leading to union with God.
Ordinance A religious ritual or practice that is understood to have been established by Jesus Christ (e.g., the Lord's Supper).
Pentecost A Jewish festival during which Jesus's apostles experienced the pouring out of the Holy Spirit (Acts 2).
Piety Actions reflecting a commitment or devotion to God in the spiritual life.
Prophecy God's message for people, communicated through an individual called a prophet.
Puritanism A Reformed Protestant movement that aimed to "purify" the English Church of its Catholic aspects. Many Puritans later separated from the Church of England.
Quietism A form of spirituality in which people wait on God, using a practice of surrender and quiet attentiveness.
Reformation A movement seeking to reform the Catholic Church, which led to the formation of the Protestant tradition.
Sacrament An outward sign, established by God, which conveys an inward or spiritual grace.

Salvation Divine action to bring humans back into right relationship with God and save them from the consequences of sin.

Sanctification The fruit of God's work within people, enabling them to reveal the divine nature in their lives.

Sin The human condition when separated from God, associated with a wide range of negative consequences.

Spiritualism A form of spirituality that emerged during the Reformation emphasizing a direct inward relationship with God, without the need for external imagery, liturgy, or sacraments.

Spirituality The various ways in which people express their religious convictions within their lives.

Tithes A tax of one-tenth of the land's produce, collected to fund the established church.

Word of God The divine power that created all things, spoke through the prophets, became flesh in Jesus Christ, and inspired the writers of the Bible.

Quaker Terms

Advices Short passages of guidance rooted in Quaker insights, used for self-examination.

Birthright Friend Someone who is born into the Quaker community.

Book of Discipline A book that sets out the agreed practices and beliefs of a Quaker body, usually a yearly meeting. It is often called "Faith and Practice."

Business Meeting A meeting for worship concerned with making decisions about the life of a Quaker community.

Clearness A term that describes the process of gaining clarity about something through spiritual discernment. Clearness committees help individual Friends gain clarity about specific decisions.

Clerks Friends appointed to ensure that business meetings are conducted in an orderly fashion, assess the "sense of the meeting," and record this in the form of a minute.

Concern An important matter or issue revealed by divine guidance that Friends may feel demands action.

Convinced Friend Someone who chooses to join the Quaker community, rather than being born into it. Traditionally, convincement meant a life-changing experience of spiritual transformation.

Disownment A decision that an individual is not in unity with the community. Those who are disowned are no longer members but can still take part in public worship.

Elders Friends who are appointed to take a particular responsibility for the spiritual life of the community. This includes ensuring that worship is conducted in good order.
Gathered Meeting A meeting for worship where those present experience a deep sense of the divine presence, binding them together and leading them.
Inward Light The presence of an inward source of inspiration and strength, often associated with the Holy Spirit.
Lamb's War Using imagery from the book of Revelation, an inward struggle to determine what guides and motivates a person's life—the Spirit of God or the spirit of the world.
Leading Divine guidance or a call to action received by individuals and communities in the context of worship or personal spiritual practice.
Ministry Giving service to the community, particularly in the form of divinely-inspired spoken messages offered within worship.
Minister A Friend who offers service to the community, particularly in the form of divinely inspired spoken messages offered within worship.
Minutes Written records describing the "sense of the meeting" in the Quaker business process. They reflect the understanding of where the Spirit has led Friends in considering a particular matter.
Monthly Meeting A Quaker community that meets monthly to do business and make decisions. In many parts of the world, this is also the weekly worshipping community.
Pastoral Care Friends who are appointed to take a particular responsibility for pastoral care within a Quaker community (formerly "overseer").
Pastoral System The practice of appointing paid pastors to undertake a range of functions within a community, including coordinating worship and pastoral care.
Programmed Worship A meeting for worship which has a pre-planned program that may include prayers, singing, music, and a sermon.
Released Friend A Friend whose ministry or concern has been recognized by their community and who receives their spiritual and practical support.
Retirement Taking time away from the normal activities of life in order to focus on the inward spiritual life and divine guidance.
Queries Questions for spiritual guidance and challenge to be considered by both individuals and communities.
Semi-Programmed Worship A meeting for worship which combines periods of open waiting and preplanned activities such as prayer, singing, and sermons.
Sense of the Meeting In a Quaker business meeting, this points to the general feeling of the people present, at any point in time, based on their discernment of where the Spirit is leading them.

Threshing Part of the discernment and decision-making process that explores one issue in detail, seeking to identify and separate out essential matters from less important ones.

Unprogrammed Worship A meeting for worship with no pre-planned order, in which people wait together in stillness and silence to experience divine guidance and revelation.

Weighty Friend Someone who is recognized for the depth of their spiritual insight and wisdom.

Yearly Meeting A large grouping of Quaker communities that meets annually to conduct business and make decisions.

Bibliography

Abbott, Margery Post. *To Be Broken and Tender: A Quaker Theology for Today.* Whittier, CA: Friend Bulletin Corporation, 2010.

Abbott, Margery Post. *Walk Humbly, Serve Boldly: Modern Quakers as Everyday Prophets.* San Francisco, CA: Inner Light Books, 2018.

Abbott, Margery Post, Mary Ellen Chijioke, Pink Dandelion, and John William Oliver, Jr., eds. *Historical Dictionary of the Friends (Quakers),* 2nd edition. Lanham, MD: Scarecrow Press, 2012.

Allen, Richard C., and Rosemary Moore, eds. *The Quakers, 1656-1723: The Evolution of an Alternative Community.* University Park, PA: The Pennsylvania State University Press, 2018.

Ambler, Rex. *The Quaker Way: A Rediscovery.* Alresford: Christian Alternative Books, 2013.

Anderson, Paul N. *Following Jesus: The Heart of Faith and Practice.* Newberg, OR: Barclay Press, 2013.

Angell, Stephen W., and Pink Dandelion, eds. *The Oxford Handbook of Quaker Studies.* Oxford: Oxford University Press, 2013.

Angell, Stephen W., and Pink Dandelion, eds. *Early Quakers and their Theological Thought.* Cambridge: Cambridge University Press, 2015.

Angell, Stephen W., and Pink Dandelion, eds. *The Cambridge Companion to Quakerism.* Cambridge: Cambridge University Press, 2018.

Angell, Stephen W., Pink Dandelion, and David Harrington Watt, eds. *The Creation of Modern Quaker Diversity, 1830–1937.* University Park, PA: The Pennsylvania State University Press, 2023.

Bacon, Margaret Hope, ed. *Wilt Thou Go on My Errand? Three 18th Century Journals of Quaker Women Ministers.* Wallingford, PA: Pendle Hill Publications, 1994.

Baisley, Phil. *The Same But Different: Ministry and the Quaker Pastor.* Richmond, IN: Friends Unite Press, 2018.

Barclay, Robert, and Licia Kuenning, ed. *An Apology for the True Christian Divinity.* Glenside, PA: Quaker Heritage Press, 2002.

Bauman, Richard. *Let Your Words be Few: Symbolism of Speaking and Silence Among Seventeenth-century Quakers.* Cambridge: Cambridge University Press, 1983.

Berk, Arthur, et al. *Traditional Quaker Christianity.* Barnesville, OH: Ohio Yearly Meeting, 2014.

Bieber, Nancy L. *Decision-Making and Spiritual Discernment: The Sacred Art of Finding Your Way.* Woodstock, VT: Skylight Paths Publishing, 2013.

Bill, J. Brent. *Holy Silence: The Gift of Quaker Spirituality.* Brewster, MA: Paraclete Press, 2005.

Bill, J. Brent. *Sacred Compass: The Way of Spiritual Discernment.* Brewster, MA: Paraclete Press, 2008.

Bill, J. Brent. *Hope and Witness in Dangerous Times: Lessons from the Quakers on Blending Faith, Daily Life, and Activism.* Alresford: Christian Alternative Books, 2021.

Birkel, Michael L. *Silence and Witness: The Quaker Tradition.* London: Darton, Longman and Todd, 2004.

Birkel, Michael L. *Engaging Scripture: Reading the Bible with Early Friends.* Richmond, IN: Friends United Press, 2005.

Bock, Cherice, and Stephen Potthoff, eds. *Quakers, Creation Care, and Sustainability: Quakers and the Disciplines*, Volume 6. Longmeadow, MA: Full Media Services, 2019.

Boulton, David, ed. *Godless for God's Sake: Nontheism in Contemporary Quakerism.* Cumbria: DHM Quaker Books, 2006.

Britain Yearly Meeting. *Quaker Faith and Practice.* London: Britain Yearly Meeting, 1994.

Brown, Peter G., and Geoffrey Garver. *Right Relationship: Building a Whole Earth Economy.* San Francisco, CA: Berrett-Koehler, 2009.

Brown, Valerie. *The Mindful Quaker: A Brief Introduction to Buddhist Wisdom for Friends.* Wallingford, PA: Pendle Hill Publications, 2006.

Buckley, Paul. *Quaker Testimony: What We Witness to the World.* Wallingford, PA: Pendle Hill Pamphlet 481, 2023.

Carey, Brycchan, and Geoffrey Plank, eds. *Quakers and Abolition.* Urbana, IL: University of Illinois Press, 2014.

Como, David. *Blown by the Spirit: Puritanism and the Emergence of an Antinomian Underground in Pre-Civil-War England.* Redwood City, CA: Stanford University Press, 2004.

Cronk, Sandra. *Dark Night Journey: Inward Re-patterning Toward a Life Centred in God*. Wallingford, PA: Pendle Hill Publications, 1991.

Dalmann, Patricia. *The Light that is Given: Prophetic Quaker Faith*. Eugene, OR: Resources Publications, 2024.

Dandelion, Pink. *The Liturgies of Quakerism*. Aldershot: Ashgate, 2004.

Dandelion, Pink. *An Introduction to Quakerism*. Cambridge: Cambridge University Press, 2007.

Dandelion, Pink. *The Quakers: A Very Short Introduction*. Oxford: Oxford University Press, 2008.

Daniels, C. Wess, and Rhiannon Grant, eds. *The Quaker World*. Abingdon: Routledge, 2022.

Dale, Jonathan, Elizabeth Cave, and Ros Morley, eds. *Faith in Action: Quaker Social Testimony*. London: Quaker Books, 2007.

Davies, Oliver. *God Within: The Mystical Tradition of Northern Europe*. New York: New City Press, 2006.

Drayton, Brian, and William P. Taber. *A Language for the Inward Landscape: Spiritual Wisdom from the Quaker Movement*. Philadelphia, PA: Tract Association of Friends, 2015.

Fager, Chuck. *Remaking Friends: How Progressive Friends Changed Quakerism & Helped Save America*. Durham, NC: CreateSpace, 2014.

Fendall, Lon, Jan Wood, and Bruce Bishop. *Practicing Discernment Together: Finding God's Way Forward in Decision-Making*. Newberg, OR: Barclay Press, 2007.

Feroli, Teresa, and Margaret Olofson, eds. *Witness, Warning and Prophecy: Quaker Women's Writings, 1655-1700*. Toronto, ON: Iter Press, 2018.

Foster Richard J. *Celebration of Discipline: The Path to Spiritual Growth*. London: Hodder and Stoughton, 2008.

Foster, Richard J., and Patricia Edwards-DeLancey. *Towards a Quaker Renaissance*. Richmond, IN: Friends United Press, 1987.

Fox, George. *The Works of George Fox*, Volumes 1–8. New York: AMS Press, 1975,

Fox, George, and John, L. Nickalls, ed. *The Journal of George Fox*. London: Quaker Books, 1997.

Glines, Elsa F. *Undaunted Zeal: The Letters of Margaret Fell*. Richmond, IN: Friends United Press, 2003.

Grant, Rhiannon. *Telling the Truth About God: Quaker Approaches to Theology.* Alresford: Christian Alternative Books, 2019.

Grant, Rhiannon. *Hearing the Light: The Core of Quaker Theology.* Alresford: Christian Alternative Books, 2021.

Gwyn, Douglas. *Apocalypse of the Word: The Life and Message of George Fox, 1624-1691.* Richmond, IN: Friends United Press, 1986.

Gwyn, Douglas. *The Covenant Crucified: Quakers and the Rise of Capitalism.* Wallingford, PA: Pendle Hill, 1995.

Gwyn, Douglas. *A Sustainable Life: Quaker Faith and Practice in the Renewal of Creation.* Philadelphia, PA: Quaker Press of FGC, 2014.

Gwyn, Douglas. *The Anti-War.* San Francisco, CA: Inner Light Books, 2016.

Hamm, Thomas D. *The Transformation of American Quakerism: Orthodox Friends, 1800-1907.* Bloomington, IN: Indiana University Press, 1988.

Healey, Robynne Rogers, ed. *Quakerism in the Atlantic World, 1690-1830.* University Park, PA: The Pennsylvania State University Press, 2021.

Heron, Alastair, ed. *Towards A Quaker View of Sex.* London: Quaker Home Service, 1964.

Hinds, Hilary. *George Fox and Early Quaker Culture.* Manchester: Manchester University Press, 2011.

Ingle, H. Larry. *First Among Friends: George Fox and the Creation of Quakerism.* Oxford: Oxford University Press, 1994.

Johns, David L. *Collected Essays of Maurice Creasey, 1912-2004.* Lampeter: Edwin Mellen Press, 2009.

Johns, David L. *Quakering Theology: Essays on Worship, Tradition and Christian Faith.* Farnham: Ashgate Publishing Limited, 2013.

Kavanagh, Jennifer. *Practical Mystics: Quaker Faith in Action.* Alresford: Christian Alternative Books, 2019.

Kavanagh, Jennifer. *Do Quakers Pray?* Alresford: Christian Alternative Books, 2023.

Kelly, Thomas. *The Eternal Promise.* Richmond, IN: Friends United Press, 1977.

Kelly, Thomas. *A Testament of Devotion.* London: Quaker Home Service, 1979.

Kennedy, Thomas C. *British Quakerism, 1860-1920: The Transformation of a Religious Community.* Oxford: Oxford University Press, 2001.

Kershner, Jon R., ed. *Quakers and Mysticism: Comparative and Syncretic Approaches to Spirituality*. Basingstoke: Palgrave Macmillan, 2019.

Lacout, Pierre. *God is Silence*. London: Friends Home Service Committee, 1970.

Loring, Patricia. *Spiritual Discernment: The Context and Goal of Clearness Committees*. Wallingford, PA: Pendle Hill Pamphlet 305, 1992.

Loring, Patricia. *Listening Spirituality: Volume I, Personal Spiritual Practices Among Friends*. Washington Grove, MD: Openings Press, 1997.

Loring, Patricia. *Listening Spirituality: Volume II, Corporate Spiritual Practices Among Friends*. Washington Grove, MD: Openings Press, 1999.

Marshall, Peter. *Reformation England, 1480-1642*. London: Bloomsbury, 2022.

Martin, Marcelle. *Our Life is Love: The Quaker Spiritual Journey*. San Francisco, CA: Inner Light Books, 2016.

Masters, Stuart. *The Rule of Christ: Themes in the Theology of James Nayler*. Leiden: Brill, 2021.

McKim, Donald K. *Westminster Dictionary of Theological Terms*. Louisville, KY: Westminster John Knox Press, 1996.

McDaniel, Donna, and Vanessa Julye. *Fit for Freedom, Not for Friendship: Quakers, African Americans, and the Myth of Racial Justice*. Philadelphia, PA: Quaker Press of Friends General Conference, 2009.

Meggitt, Justin J. *Early Quakers and Islam: Slavery, Apocalyptic and Christian-Muslim Encounters in the Seventeenth Century*. Uppsala: Swedish Science Press, 2013.

Mombo, Esther, and Cecile Nyiramana. *Mending Broken Hearts, Rebuilding Shattered Lives: Quaker Peacemaking in East and Central Africa*. London: Quaker Books, 2016.

Moore, Rosemary. *The Light in their Consciences: Early Quakers in Britain, 1646-1666*. University Park, PA: Pennsylvania State University Press, 2000.

Moyer, Paul B. *The Public Universal Friend: Jemima Wilkinson and Religious Enthusiasm in Revolutionary America*. Ithaca, NY: Cornell University Press, 2015.

Muers, Rachel. *Keeping God's Silence: Towards a Theological Ethics of Communication*. Oxford: Wiley-Blackwell, 2004.

Muers, Rachel. *Testimony: Quakerism and Theological Ethics.* London: SCM Press, 2015.

Nayler, James, and Licia Kuenning, ed. *The Works of James Nayler,* Volumes 1-4. Glenside, PA: Quaker Heritage Press, 2003-2009.

North Carolina Yearly Meeting (Conservative). *Faith and Practice.* Greensboro, NC: North Carolina Yearly Meeting Conservative, 1983.

Ohio Yearly Meeting (Conservative). *The Book of Discipline.* Barnesville, OH: Ohio Yearly Meeting Conservative, 2001.

Palmer, Parker J. *The Promise of Paradox: A Celebration of Contradictions in the Christian Life.* Notre Dame, IN: Ave Maria Press.1980.

Palmer, Parker J. *The Active Life: A Spirituality of Work, Creativity, and Caring.* San Francisco, CA: Jossey Bass, 1999.

Palmer, Parker J. *Let Your Life Speak: Listening for the Voice of Vocation.* San Francisco, CA: Jossey Bass, 2000.

Palmer, Parker J. *Hidden Wholeness: The Journey Toward and Undivided Life.* San Francisco, CA: Jossey Bass, 2004.

Penn, William. *No Cross, No Crown: A Discourse, Showing the Nature and Discipline of the Holy Cross of Christ.* York: Sessions, 1981.

Punshon, John. *Encounter with Silence: Reflections from the Quaker Tradition.* Richmond, IN: Friends United Press, 1987.

Punshon, John. *Testimony and Tradition: Some Aspects of Quaker Spirituality.* London: Quaker Home Service, 1990.

Punshon, John. *Reasons for Hope: The Faith and Future of the Friends Church.* Richmond, IN: Friends United Press, 2001.

Rediker, Marcus. *The Fearless Benjamin Lay: The Quaker Dwarf Who Became the First Revolutionary Abolitionist.* Boston, MA: Beacon Press, 2017.

Roth, John D., and James M. Stayer, eds. *A Companion to Anabaptism and Spiritualism, 1521–1700.* Leiden: Brill, 2007.

Russ, Mark. *Quaker-Shaped Christianity: How the Jesus Story and the Quaker Way Fit Together.* Alresford: Christian Alternative Books, 2022.

Scully, Jackie Leach, and Pink Dandelion, eds. *Good and Evil: Quaker Perspectives.* Aldershot: Ashgate, 2007.

Sheeran, Michael J. *Beyond Majority Rule: Voteless Decisions in the Religious Society of Friends.* Philadelphia, PA: Philadelphia Yearly Meeting, 1996.

Smith, Nigel. *Perfection Proclaimed: Language and Literature in English Radical Religion, 1640-1669.* Oxford: Clarendon, 1989.

Snyder, C. Arnold. *Following in the Footsteps of Christ: The Anabaptist Tradition.* London: Darton, Longman & Todd, 2004.

Spencer, Carole Dale. *Holiness: The Soul of Quakerism.* Milton Keynes: Paternoster Press, 2007.

Swann, Laura. *The Wisdom of the Beguines: The Forgotten Story of a Medieval Women's Movement.* Katonah, NY: Blue Bridge, 2014.

Taber, William. *Four Doors into Meeting for Worship.* Wallingford, PA: Pendle Hill Pamphlet 306, 1992.

Trueblood, D. Elton. *The People Called Quakers: The Enduring Influence of a Way of Life and a Way of Thought.* New York: Harper & Row, 1966.

Wallace, Terry S. *A Sincere and Constant Love: An Introduction to the Work of Margaret Fell.* Richmond, IN: Friends United Press, 1992.

Ward, Madeleine. *The Christian Quaker: George Keith and the Keithian Controversy.* Leiden: Brill, 2019.

Weaver, Harold D. Kries, Paul, and Stephen W. Angell, eds. *Black Fire: African American Quakers on Spirituality and Human Rights.* Philadelphia, PA: Quaker Press of FGC, 2011.

Wilcox, Catherine M. *Theology and Women's Ministry in Seventeenth Century English Quakerism: Handmaidens of the Lord.* Lampeter: Edwin Mellen Press, 1995.

Willcuts, Jack L. *Why Friends are Friends: Some Quaker Core Convictions Practice.* Newberg, OR: Barclay Press, 1984.

Williams, George Huntston. *The Radical Reformation*, 3rd edition. Kirksville, MO: Truman State University Press, 2000.

Wilson, Lloyd Lee. *Essays on the Quaker Vision of Gospel Order.* Burnsville, NC: Celo Valley Books, 1993.

Woolman, John, and Phillips P. Moulton, ed. *The Journal and Major Essays of John Woolman.* Richmond, IN: Friends United Press, 1989.

Index

Note: Page locators followed by 'n.' refer to notes.

abolitionism   120, 162
accountability   112–13
Act of Uniformity   35
Adam   20, 27
Advent   78
Africa   53, 54, 125
African Americans   120, 126, 162
Alternatives to Violence
    Project   124
America   39, 46, 48, 52, 120, 162
Anabaptists   11, 12
animals, 107, 111, 115
Anthony, Susan B.   48
apocalyptic   15, 30, 68, 69
Apology (Barclay)   39
apostles, the   9, 23, 108, 170
Atiamuga, Maria   54
atonement   46, 47

baptism   24, 25, 51
Barclay, Robert   23, 37, 39, 49, 77, 159
Benezet, Anthony   44
Bible, the   2, 5, 10, 22–3, 30, 43, 45–7, 49, 54, 83, 97, 101, 138, 149
Blackborow, Sarah   116
Bolivia   53, 123
Book of Discipline   70
born again   19, 20
Boulton, David   58
Braxton-Hicks   173
British Empire   38, 40, 119
British Friends   52
British Quaker   51, 58
British Quaker project   125
Bryant and May   160

Buddhism   81–2
Burnell, Jocelyn Bell   2
Burrough, Edward   69
business meetings   163

Cadbury, George   121
Calvinism   39
Caribbean, the   119, 161
Cassian, John   92
Catholic Church   9, 10
Catholicism, Roman   12, 66
Cazden, Elizabeth   161
Celebration of Discipline (Foster)   87
charismatic   28, 29, 38, 40, 59, 60, 67, 93, 122, 153
Charles I, King   13
Charles II, King   21, 30, 35, 36, 39
Cheevers, Sarah   15
Christendom   11, 167
Christian Church   87, 92, 169
Christian faith   19, 31, 87
Christianity   1, 18, 25, 117, 148, 152, 168, 169
Christians   17, 51, 68, 169
Christian worship   66
Christ indwelling   116
Christ in Spirit   24–5, 29
Church, the   9, 12, 18, 21, 23–4, 26, 31, 93
Church of England   12, 35, 117, 159
Civil War
    American   120
    English   1, 13
class   158, 160, 161
clearness committees   105–6
clergy   21, 70, 156
clerk   100, 101

colonialism   95, 124, 126
Commonwealth, English   13
communion, holy   24, 51, 71, 85
communitarian   59, 60
community   3, 4, 19, 27, 36, 40, 43,
    55, 67, 72, 86, 92, 93, 99
community testimony   114
concerns   31, 37, 44, 76, 83, 112, 115
conscientious objection   124
Conservative Friends   59, 98, 148,
    169, 172
contemplation   135, 137
contemplative   2, 18, 23, 28, 42
contemplative prayer   43, 76
contemplative spirituality   170
conversion   11, 45
convincement   20
covenant
    new   17, 23–6, 117, 118, 149
    old   17, 18, 117
creation
    new   5, 17, 68, 143–5, 150
    original   27, 82, 111
Creeds   25, 148
Cromwell, Oliver   13, 15, 35
Cross, The   142

Dalton, John   2
dead faith   117, 118
decision-making   36, 91, 93,
    98–101, 104
devotional writings   77–9
discernment   4, 112, 138, 139
    awareness   95–6
    within Christianity   92–3
    and decision-making   98–9
    honesty   96
    individual discernment   104
    ministry   102
    nature   94
    as personal practice   103
    practice   94
    spiritual gifts   102–3
    and spirituality   91–2

threshing meeting   101–2
    and traditional Quaker
        spirituality   93–4
discipline   3, 4, 12, 19, 27, 28, 40, 42,
    56, 72, 76, 77, 91, 99, 103, 138
disownment   42, 119
distinctive faith   3, 22–5
divine command   108, 168
divine guidance   3, 84, 92, 99, 108,
    110, 140
divine indwelling   20, 55
divine power   136
divine presence   71, 74–6, 168
doctrine   37, 45, 52, 55, 167
dynamic tension   147, 150–2, 154–8

early Quaker movement   13–16, 18,
    28, 30, 31, 152, 167
early Quaker testimony   21, 117,
    118, 123
East African Quaker Profiles   54
Eastern Orthodoxy   66, 76
ecological crisis   126
ecology   126
Eddington, Arthur   2
elders   72, 100, 101, 103
endogamy   41, 119
end times, the   14, 53, 70
England   1, 12, 15, 39, 151, 156
English Reformation   12–13
English Revolution   3, 37, 68
enslavement   38, 119, 161, 162
epistles   78, 101
equality   54, 55
    spiritual   37, 116, 127
    testimony   114, 115
Eternal Being   143
Eucharist   66, 71, 85
European Reformation   3, 10–11
Evangelical Christians   2, 49, 87,
    171
Evangelical Friends   48, 50–2, 59,
    83, 85, 98, 122, 126, 148, 149,
    152–6, 171

Evangelical Friends Church 51, 125, 152, 154
Evangelicalism 45–9, 52, 86, 120
Evangelical mission 52–3, 123
Evangelical movement 4, 51, 83
Evangelical Quakers 51, 83, 86–7, 160
Evangelical Revivalism 48, 154
Evans, Katherine 15
Everarde, John 13
evil 30, 35, 101, 155, 161

faith 5, 11, 16, 17, 28, 48, 80, 140, 142–3, 148, 168
  Christian 19, 20, 31
  community 156, 157, 170
  dead 117, 118
  distinctive 3, 22–5
  lived 20–2, 97, 117–18, 152
  radical 26–7
  tradition 57
Fell, Margaret 14, 15, 22, 27, 30, 116, 161
Fisher, Mary 15
Foster, Richard J. 87
Fothergill, John 2
Fox, George 14, 15, 21, 27, 36, 38, 39, 111, 112, 151, 161
Franklin, Ursula 2
Friends of Color 162
Fry, Elizabeth 121

Gay Friends 42
gender identity 57, 122, 126–7
Gentiles 18, 37, 101
gifts 72, 102, 154, 170
Global South 53, 86, 87, 123
gospel order 94
government 27, 125
Grindletonians 13
Grubb, Edward 122
Gurney, Joseph John 45, 48, 49
Gurneyite Friends 51

Healing and Rebuilding Our Communities 125
heaven 18, 53, 54, 93
heaven on earth 109, 126
Hebrews, Letter to the 17
hell 53, 54
Henry VIII 12
Hicks, Elias 45, 47
Hicksite Friends 47
Hicksite-Orthodox separation 46–7
holiness 2, 13, 43, 51, 155
Holiness Revival movement 50
Holy Communion 47, 51, 71, 74, 85
Holy Saturday 78
Holy Spirit 10, 11, 19, 25, 27, 29, 35, 41, 46, 49, 55, 66, 70, 73, 78, 92, 97, 98, 112, 143, 154, 167
Hookes, Ellis 156
Hopkins, Johns 2
Howgill, Francis 69
human authority 70, 149
human fallibility 155
humanity 10, 18, 35, 83, 94, 172
human motivation 43, 92
human sexuality 126, 127
human transformation 19–20

idolatry 65
Incarnation, the 17
individualism 31, 103, 139
individual spiritual practices 19, 87–8
integrity testimony 114
Inward Light 39, 47–9, 138
Ireland 1, 15, 51
Irish Quakers 51

Jeremiah, The prophet 17
Jesus Christ 17, 18, 20, 31, 65, 66, 70, 93
Jews 17, 18, 37
John, The Gospel of 23
Jones, Rufus 56

journals 77, 87
*The Just and Equal Balance
    Discovered* (Blackborow) 116
justification 46, 49, 50, 61 n.15

Keith, George 39
Keithian controversy 38–9
Kelly, Thomas 76
Kenya 52–4, 123
King, Martin Luther, Jr. 126
King, Sallie 82
Kingdom of God 35, 109, 150, 173

Lamb's War 30, 36
leadings 3, 23, 26, 76, 98, 112, 114, 120, 141, 168
Liberal Christians 59
Liberal Friends 55, 59–60, 98, 123, 127, 149, 152
Liberalism 120
Liberal Protestant theology 54–5
Liberal Quaker 148, 155, 156, 169
    culture 60
    meetings 152
    pluralist Liberal Quaker 58, 80–3
    profiles 55–6
Light, the 74, 75, 134, 135, 137
listening 27, 79, 93, 99, 100, 105, 113, 168
Lister, Joseph 2
liturgical year 25, 78
liturgy 10, 21, 71, 85, 117, 147
living faith 20–2, 97, 117–18, 152
London 41
London Yearly Meeting 47
Luffe, John 15
Lung'aho, Daudi 54

Manchester Conference 52
Maniraguha, Solange 125
Maraga, Maria 54
marriage 41, 53, 119
medieval period 9

mental health 122
Methodism 46
Methodist revival movement 45, 46
ministers 21, 24, 43, 45, 53, 55, 69
ministry 24, 102, 156
    public 26, 116
    as service 102
    as spoken 43, 99
minutes 100–1
mission 4, 14, 39, 51, 52, 123
modernism 52, 54, 59, 81, 82, 122, 154
Mohammed IV, Sultan 15
Mombo, Esther 124, 125
Morris, Susanna 43
Mott, Lucretia 48
music 73, 86, 87
Mutua, Rasoah 54
Mweresa, Gideon W. H. 87
mysticism 55, 56

Native Americans 44, 48
Nayler, James 14, 15, 23, 30, 37, 115
negative testimony 109–11
new millennium 58–9
New Testament 29, 78, 93, 101
nominations 102, 103
Nontheism 58, 82–3
North America 1, 51–3, 86, 160, 161
Nyiramana, Cecile 124, 125

oaths 21
open worship 85
orchestral metaphor 73
Orthodox Friends 47, 48, 56
Orthodox Quakerism 48
Osborne, William 22

Paganism 82
Parliament 35, 36
Pastoral Friends 59, 83, 148, 153, 156
Pastoral system 50–1

pastors 50, 53, 84–6, 156
patriarchy 26, 116
Paul, the apostle 23, 31, 37, 68, 76, 92, 102, 140
peacebuilding 122, 124
peace testimony 113–14
peculiarity 40–2, 50, 51, 169
penal reform 121–2
Penn, William 39, 121
Pennington, Isaac 28
Pennsylvania 39, 121, 162
Pentecost 17
Pentecostal 15, 68, 86, 93, 154
The People Called Quakers (Trueblood) 169
perfection 20, 155
Perrot, John 15
persecution 4, 11, 36, 37, 116, 158, 163
Peter, the apostle 17
Philadelphia 41, 42
philanthropic people 119–22
philanthropy 45, 121, 159
pilgrimage 139
Plain Friends 42
plainness 41, 47, 49, 119
pluralism 57, 58, 81, 152
Pluralist Liberal Friends 56–7, 80–1
Pluralist Liberal Quakerism 80–1
Pluralist Quaker 57, 169, 172
political lobbying 36, 125
positive testimony 109–10
practice, spiritual, *see* spiritual practices
prayer 43, 76, 85, 87
predestination 12, 13
primitive Christianity 22, 46, 168, 171
programmed worship 47
Progressive Friends 120
prophecy 72, 93
prophets, the 23, 157, 162
Protestantism 46
Protestant Reformation 2, 66

Protestants 10, 71, 85, 93, 170
purification 20
Puritan/Puritanism 12–14, 25, 118
 family 14
 radical 12, 13, 15, 151
 reformed 23

Quaker 1, 21, *see also individual entries*
 conviction 43, 108, 122, 171
 community 36, 40, 41, 50, 51, 53, 119, 123, 157, 171
 Conservative 59, 98, 148, 169, 172
 culture 160
 diplomacy 125
 discipline 44
 Evangelical 48, 50–2, 59, 83–5, 98, 122, 126, 149, 152–6, 171
 faith 49
 Liberal (*see* Liberal Quaker)
 mission 51
 movement 9, 31, 35, 37, 53, 172
 nontheism 58
 organization 98
 Pastoral 59, 83, 148, 153, 156
 pluralist 56–7, 80–1, 169, 172
 profiles 45–6
 rejection 158, 167
 sectarianism 150
 spiritual heritage 2
 spirituality 3, 38, 56, 69, 106, 107, 155
 universalists 57–8
Quaker Act of 1662 36
Quaker Council for European Affairs (QCEA) 125
Quaker diversity
 individualist-communitarian tension 31–2
 quietist-charismatic tension 28–9
 separatist-activist tension 30–1

universalist-christian
  tension   29–30
Quaker Oats Company   1
Quaker testimony   5, 107, 123, 127
  accountability   112–13
  community testimony   114
  divine command   108
  equality testimony   114, 115
  heaven on Earth   109
  humans and creation   111
  integrity testimony   114
  missional and campaigning
    people   122–7
  mutual support   112
  negative testimony   109–10
  nonviolent communication   112
  peace testimony   113–14
  peculiar people   117
  philanthropic people   119–22
  positive testimony   109–10
  radical people   115–16
  right conduct   115
  right focus   115
  right relationship   115
  simplicity testimony   113
  stewardship testimony   114–15
  way of Jesus   108–9
Quaker United Nations Office
  (QUNO)   125
Quaker Universalist Group   57
Quietism   45, 48
Quietist   18, 28, 40, 47, 59, 152, 153
quietist-charismatic tension   28–9
Quietist Friends   43, 47
Quietist period   40, 41, 43
Quietist Quaker profiles   44
Quietist spirituality   42–4
quiet waiting   75–6, 85

racism   126, 162
radical faith   26–7
radical Puritan movement   13
rationalism   45, 56, 134
recorded ministers   72, 103

Reformation
  English   12–13, 37
  European   3, 10–11
  radical   12
reformers, the   10
Restoration, the   16, 35, 42
resurrection   20, 78
revelation   27, 55, 68, 145, 151
  divine   3, 96
Revivalism   48, 50–1
Richmond Declaration   51, 84
Roman Catholic Church   12
Rowntree, John Wilhelm   55, 56
Rustin, Bayard   126

Sabbath   18
sacraments   10, 24–5, 47, 85
salvation   10, 11, 13, 32 n.2, 49, 50,
  59, 155
sanctification   46, 49, 50
Schimmelpenninck, Mary
  Anne   159
Scriptures   13, 23, 48, 49, 54, 55, 77,
  97, 101
seekers   14, 68
self-centeredness   139, 144
semi-programmed worship   84
separations   11, 30, 39, 41, 46–50,
  123, 148
sexuality   53, 126
signs, prophetic   15
simplicity testimony   113
sin   30, 87, 115, 136, 155
Snell, Beatrix Saxon   73
social inequality   37, 158
South America   51, 53, 86, 123
spirit, diagnosis   136
Spirit of Christ   21, 109
spiritual awareness   57, 134
spiritual empowerment   15, 153
spiritual equality   37, 116, 127
spiritual freedom   154
spiritual gifts   102–3
spiritual heritage   2, 134

Spiritualists 11
spiritual journey 133, 138
spiritual practices 3, 4, 19, 20, 27, 38, 44, 65, 74–5, 82
   contemplative prayer 76
   devotional writings 77–9
   quiet waiting 75–6
   stillness 79–80
   testimony 141
   times of retirement 76–7
   tuning in 78–9
   waiting 78
Stanton, Elizabeth Cady 48
stewardship testimony 114–15
Summer Schools movement 56
Swarthmoor Hall 14

temperance 121
testimony, *see* Quaker testimony
threshing meeting 101–2
tithes 21, 117
To All the Nations under the Whole Heavens (Fox) 21
toleration, religious 36, 39, 161
Tomlinson, Ambrose Jessup 154
Towards a Quaker View of Sex (Heron) 127
tradition 3, 5, 55, 57, 66, 81, 86, 127, 149, 151, 153
traditional Quaker approach 72, 73, 80, 84, 94, 148
Trinity, The 66
Trueblood, Elton 169
Turning the Tide 125

universalism 29, 57, 81, 152
universalist-christian tension 29–30
Unprogrammed Friends 153
unprogrammed worship 19, 67, 68, 70–4, 84

violence 3, 110, 118
vita apostolica 9, 11

waiting 19, 28, 43, 46, 49, 66–70, 73, 74, 78, 143
Wesley, John 44
Western Christianity 2, 170
Western Quaker community 53
Wilbur, John 45, 46, 48
Wilburite-Gurneyite separation 48–50
Wimber, John 154
women 26, 48
   ministry of 37, 54
   position 163–4
   spiritual equality 116, 127
Women's Speaking Justified (Fell) 116
Woodbrooke settlement 56
Woolman, John 29, 44, 77
worship 4, 27, 43, 65, 67–8
   for church affairs 99
   communal worship 19, 27, 67, 81
   in East Africa 86
   in Global South 86, 87
   individual spiritual practices 19, 87–8
   meetings 72
   in North America 86
   open worship 85
   practice 2, 66, 67
   programmed 84
   semi-programmed 84
   in South America 86
   unprogrammed 19, 67, 68, 70–4, 84

About the Author

Stuart K. Masters is a teacher and writer with a focus on the Quaker faith, its history, theology, spirituality and relationship with other traditions. For fifteen years, he worked for Woodbrooke, an international Quaker learning and research organization based in Britain, and following his retirement, continues to offer courses and events as an Associate Tutor. His book, *The Rule of Christ: Themes in the Theology of James Nayler*, was published by Brill in June 2021. He is a Regional Representative for the Anabaptist Mennonite Network, and a member of the Advisory Council for the American Journal, *Quaker Religious Thought*.

www.ingramcontent.com/pod-product-compliance
Ingram Content Group UK Ltd.
Pitfield, Milton Keynes, MK11 3LW, UK
UKHW022136220426
470275UK00006B/85